The SHACKLETON VOYAGES

The SHACKLETON VOYAGES

Introduced by ROLAND HUNTFORD

Picture research and captions by JULIE SUMMERS

Design and art direction by DAVID ROWLEY

TED SMART

'I have often been asked what one can see in the cold, inhospitable regions of the Antarctic? And confronted by a bold question such as that, it is hard to find an answer . . .

'Ever since we were last there we have thought and dreamed of the wild stretches of snow and ice, the silence of those places where men never trod before, the wonder of the unknown as it rolled into our ken. Those are the memories that remain, and not the bitter cold, the hard work, the rough and often scanty food, and the constant effort to do just a little more than one should expect.'

From 'Go I Must – The Call of the Antarctic' by Sir Ernest Shackleton, *Daily Mail*, 31 December 1913

Introduction

One day in March 1909 a sturdy figure strode into a telegraph office on Stewart Island, off the coast of New Zealand. His name was Ernest Shackleton. In the harbour lay the low dark ship that had just brought him back from Antarctica. He handed over a cable with echoes of the distant past: the mantle of Protesilaios had descended upon Shackleton. Protesilaios – 'Great-hearted Protesilaios' as Homer calls him – is one of the melancholy figures of classical mythology. He was the first man from the Greek fleet to set foot on land at the start of the Trojan War. He was also the first to fall and embodies the tragic fate of the pioneer: he who shows the way only for others to triumph in his stead.

What Shackleton said in his cable was that he had tried to be the first man at the South Pole, and failed in the attempt. He had set a record for the Furthest South, but that was scant consolation. The bitter prospect was that someone else would reap the fruit of all his striving. Robert Falcon Scott and Roald Amundsen, rivals for the Pole, were waiting in the wings.

Shackleton's world was very different from ours. It did not have the view from space. The vision of the earth was still bounded by the horizon, as it had been for our primitive ancestors. The surface of the globe was not yet fully explored. Antarctica was the last great blank upon the map. The interior was hardly known at all. Even the coast was a mystery in parts. Shackleton had trodden where no one else had been before. In so doing, he was playing his part in the last act of the age of terrestrial discovery.

Symbolical geographic goals had arisen to mark the process. The sources of the Nile, the Northwest Passage and the Northeast Passage were among the more romantic. All these challenges had been overcome. What remained in Shackleton's day were the last emblems of the ultimate: the highest mountain, the poles of the earth. But it was these last two that had the power to obsess. Neither the North nor South Pole had yet been conquered. While Shackleton was making his attempt in Antarctica, at the opposite end of the earth, men were aiming to be the first at the magic point of 90° North latitude. But each of these extremes was hidden from the other, for this was before the age of instant global communication.

By now the telegraph and submarine cable did indeed encircle the globe, but access depended on the cablehead. Radio did exist, but not yet universally. When explorers sailed over the horizon, they were lost

to the world, while they for their part felt an isolation which today seems inconceivable. Even the first astronauts, in constant touch with their control centres, were not as lonely as they.

In consequence, of crucial importance to the leader of every expedition, was bringing the news to market. Hence the race to reach the cablehead. That meant almost as much as the race for the goal itself. The headlines were half the battle. The scoop was all. This was Shackleton's concern when he entered the cable office on Stewart Island. He had timed his landfall so that the cable would make the first edition of the *Daily Mail,* with whom he had a contract to provide his exclusive story. There was an impact in all this denied to us, in the age of instant communication. Today, with mild interest, we follow our adventurers' every move in all the media, almost as though we were with them. But when Shackleton went ashore on Stewart Island, he was like someone returning from the dead. The world had had to wait for months to learn about the deed. Aviation was in its infancy. Louis Blériot had not yet flown the English Channel. The ocean liner still linked the continents – no jetting here and there. Shackleton took more than two and a half months to make his way from Stewart Island back to England. When he arrived, he burst upon a public that was frenzied and expectant – and was transformed at a stroke into the quintessential Edwardian hero.

Like other explorers, in a very real sense Shackleton was above all the creation of the press. More exactly, he was projected through the medium of the press photograph, which was now just coming into its own. But here again the impact was delayed. In Shackleton's time the wire-photo was unknown. The first pictures had to await the post. For this reason, they were weeks behind the cable, but when they did arrive the sensation they created could be huge. They did not have to compete with the fluid continuity of television, but revived and reinforced the earlier reports.

The still photograph by definition captures the moment. It has a single point of focus. It says something not only about the subject but the eye behind the lens, and hence the inner story of the age. Shackleton's pictures did this with astounding effect. When at last they arrived, his strange heavy-browed eyes, radiating sheer force of personality, stared out at the reader of every newspaper and magazine with overwhelming power.

A triumphant Shackleton in London following his return from the Furthest South. He loved the camera and the camera loved Shackleton. During the summer of 1909 his face appeared in almost every newspaper and regularly in magazines. As he became a familiar face, his popularity as a national hero grew.

South Georgia

Coronation Island

Clarence Island
Elephant Island   Joinville Island

Snow Hill Island

Snow Island
Deception Island

Tierra del Fuego   Larsen
                                                   Ice Shelf
                        Antarctic   Graham
                        Peninsula   Land   Lassiter Coast

South   Alexander Island
America

                                                    Bellingshausen Sea

Pacific
Ocean
                                                              Amundsen Sea

Antarctic Circle

Weddell Sea

Stancomb Wills
Promontory

Vahsel
Bay

Princess Martha
Coast

Caird Coast

Luitpold Coast

Filchner
Ice Shelf

40°   30°   20°   10°   0°

50°

60°

70°

80°

90°

45°   50°   100°   55°   110°   60°   120°   65°   130°   140°

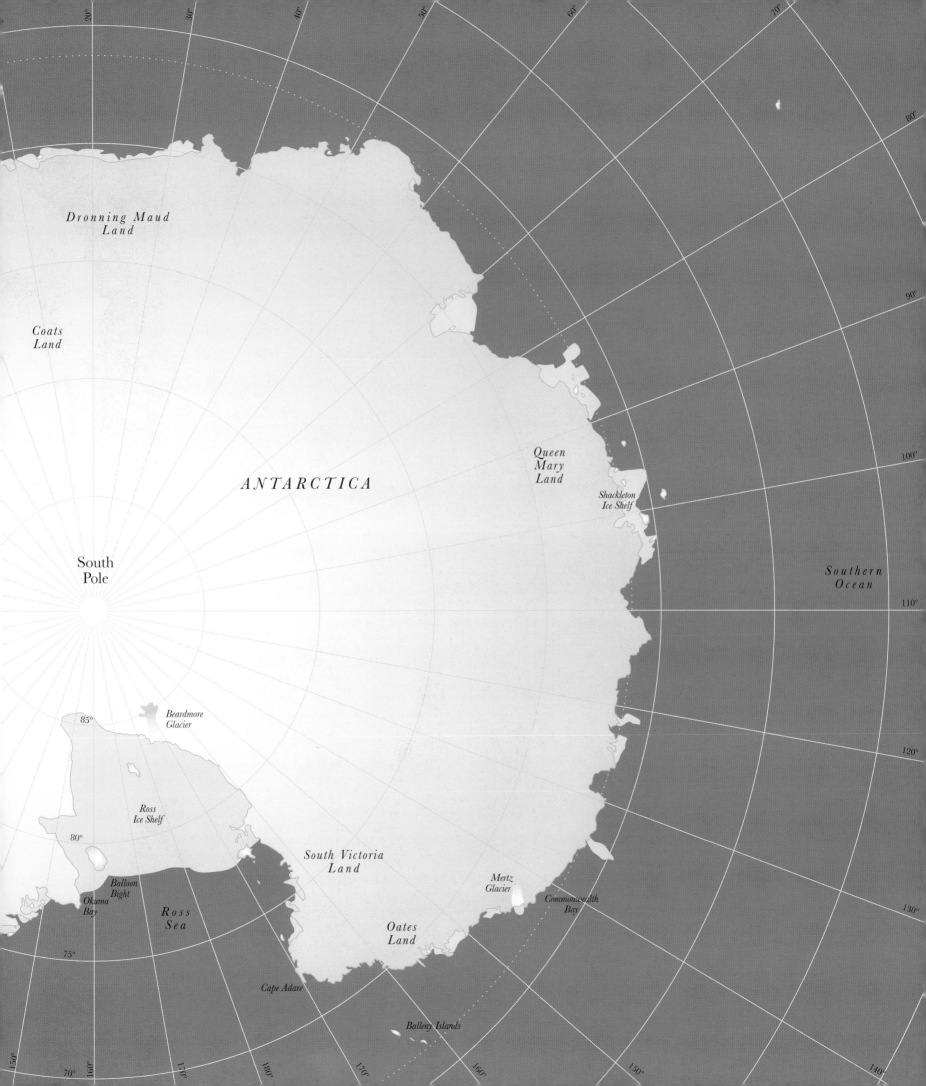

THE EARLY YEARS AND
THE MERCANTILE MARINE

Opposite: On 19 April 1890 Shackleton, at the age of sixteen, joined Hoghton Tower *in Liverpool.*
Right: 'Troopin', Troopin', Troopin' to the Sea.' "O.H.M.S.", *Shackleton's first published work, was an illustrated record of the voyage of S.S.* Tintagel Castle *conveying 1,200 soldiers from Southampton to Cape Town, March 1900.*

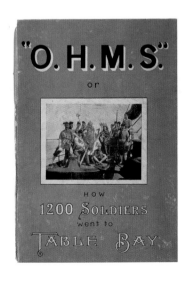

Born on 15 February 1874, Ernest Henry Shackleton had a late-Victorian upbringing. His father was a doctor, and he lived in the respectable south London suburb of Sydenham. The second child, he had eight sisters and a younger brother. After the usual preliminaries of governess and preparatory school, Shackleton went to public school. In this instance it was Dulwich College, two hundred years old and nearby, which he attended as a day boy. On the face of it, Shackleton seemed a good average specimen of his kind and class, even down to the size of his family.

Appearances were deceptive. Shackleton was born in Ireland, at Kilkea, in County Kildare. He was Anglo-Irish, that conveniently forgotten breed, the Protestant Ascendancy of English stock and rootless on that account. In Ireland the Anglo-Irish were despised as alien rulers; in England not quite accepted but patronised as Irish of sorts. Shackleton was an outsider from the start. It did not help that his family had been in Ireland for generations, and that his father had moved to England in search of better times.

Like most outsiders, Shackleton felt indefinably ill at ease, with behaviour to match. He was quick-witted and intelligent, but an unwilling pupil. In 1890, at the age of sixteen, through impulse or ambition, he left school early and went to sea. He did so with the connivance of his father – no moralising paterfamilias, but an admirable realist, with a talent for survival.

Shackleton started off in sail, before the mast. His first voyages were the stuff of schoolboy tales – on a full-rigger, round Cape Horn, with much going aloft on swaying ratlines, 'one hand for the ship and one for himself', in storms violently rolling the mast from side to side. This was his apprenticeship to the sea. Eventually he graduated to steam. He rose to become a merchant officer. In 1898, at the age of twenty-four, he obtained his Master's certificate, which entitled him to captain any British ocean-going ship – in theory at least. In practice, the situation was different.

So far, Shackleton had been on tramp ships, as Second or Third Mate, roaming the world where the cargoes took him. Restless, forceful, with something of the wanderer, already seemingly at home only on the deck of a ship at sea, but with a strong touch of the wayward, he seemed to have found a way of life wholly in conformity with his character. Then in 1899, he left the tramping trade. Through an old school friend, he joined the Union Castle Line. This ran the mail ships to South Africa. It was an institution of

The Ship and her Officers.

Surgeon
W. McLean.

Third Officer
E. H. Shackleton.

Second Officer
T. Tenison.

Fourth Officer
A. E. W. Cripps.

Purser
R. W. Evans.

Chief Officer
J. M. Anderson.

Captain
R. F. Harris

Chief Engineer
D. Collier.

THE COMMANDER AND OFFICERS OF S.S. "TINTAGEL CASTLE."

Empire. Greatly desirable, it was difficult to enter. It was far from the vagaries of tramp ships. Its vessels ran to a timetable, regularly returning home. What is more, Shackleton was no longer dealing with cargo, but in potentially useful passengers. He soon progressed from Fourth to Third Officer.

That same year the Boer War broke out, and Shackleton found himself serving on Union Castle troop ships. On one of them, he met Cedric Longstaff, a British Army lieutenant. Longstaff's father, Llewellyn Longstaff, had made the biggest private donation to an Antarctic expedition then being organised in England. Shackleton decided to join it. Through the father's influence and his acquaintance with the son, he succeeded in doing so.

2

3

2 Henrietta Letitia Sophia Gavan married Henry Shackleton in 1872. For the first years of her marriage she provided the family with a happy, secure home. However, when the family moved to England, having borne her husband ten children, she developed a mysterious illness, which confined her to her sick room for the last forty years of her life. After that she played little active role in her children's lives; they were brought up by their father, their maternal grandmother and a string of visiting female relatives from Ireland, who came over periodically to help out.

1, 3 Henry Shackleton, Ernest's father, had begun his career as a farmer in Ireland, but a disastrous agricultural depression coupled with the need to feed his large young family led him to retrain, at the age of thirty-three, as a doctor. He moved to Britain in 1884, immediately after qualifying, and practised as a GP in Sydenham for the rest of his life. A non-conformist in many ways, Henry Shackleton practised homeopathy. He was described by one of his patients as being 'very kind and gentle' in spite of his 'alarming beard'.

1

1 Aberdeen House, the Shackleton house in
Sydenham, where the family lived from
1885, was in a respectable part of southeast
London, close to Crystal Palace and all the
entertainment it had to offer. Dr Shackleton
took great pride in his magnificent rose
garden at the back of the house and the
children were able to enjoy the switch-back
slide that Ernest constructed from the back
wall across the lawn.

2 The front drawing-room of Aberdeen
House, Sydenham had a fireplace with the
Shackleton family arms carved above it.

3 Dulwich College c.1886. Shackleton is sitting
at the back of the group in the window. He
attended Dulwich College until 1889 and
although not academically gifted, he did
better in English history and literature than
his close friends Burne and Petrides.

2

3

'I came to be drawn to the reading of history – I mean a certain type of history. I was never much taken with records of battles and sieges, and dynasties . . . but . . . of adventurous nations who sent their mariners into unknown seas, and the history of colonisation and exploration . . . I was more or less acquainted from my earliest youth with all the problems of exploration, whether in Central Africa . . . Tibet, the North and South Poles . . . I not only read . . . but remembered what I had read. I may truly say that long before I went to the Antarctic myself I knew everything and everybody that had been before me, to either end of the earth's axis.'

'How I began', interview with Shackleton in *The Captain*, April 1910

Although Shackleton's father was reluctant to give his son permission to leave school early, Shackleton joined the mercantile marine at the age of sixteen. The myth that he ran away to sea was probably generated by Shackleton himself.

SOUTH WITH SCOTT ON DISCOVERY 1901-3

Opposite: Shackleton dressed in sledging gear, 1902.
Right: The South Polar Times *was typed and edited by Shackleton and illustrated by Dr Edward Wilson. It was launched on 23 April 1903, the day 'the sun disappeared from our view for 121 days and the long Antarctic winter . . . commenced'.*

THE SOUTH POLAR TIMES 1902-3.

"DISCOVERY"

On the face of it, this seemed improbable: Shackleton appeared to have settled down to a career. Further promotion seemed only a matter of time. However, behind those stern, expressive features, and within that squat, muscular frame, smouldered ambition. Shackleton had quickly become restless with routine. The merchant service was too small for him. He was in a hurry to succeed. He wanted a short cut to glory, and the riches he expected to follow in its train. An Antarctic expedition appeared providentially as the opening he sought.

So on 6 August 1901, Shackleton sailed down the Channel and watched the coast of England sink astern from the deck of *Discovery*, the expedition ship. Four other expeditions, from Sweden, Germany, France and Scotland, were also heading south. After a long lapse, Antarctic exploration was in the process of revival. Patriotism was the real drive.

The explorer as hero was an established figure in the West. In the latter part of the nineteenth century, 'Darkest Africa' had held the stage. But once the source of the Nile, the most celebrated of the geographical goals, had been settled by another creation of the press, Henry Morton Stanley, in 1877, and the continent carved up by the European colonial powers, that region had lost its fascination. There remained the Poles. Around Stanley's time, the Swedish-speaking Finn, Professor Baron Adolf Erik Nordenskiöld, had become the first to navigate the Northeast Passage, the legendary route between the Atlantic and the Pacific along the Arctic coast of Siberia, and the first to circumnavigate the Old World into the bargain. He was the sensation of the hour.

It was the Norwegian Fridtjof Nansen, however, who established himself as the true polar hero by being the first to cross Greenland in 1888 and, above all, through his drift across the Arctic in *Fram* between 1893 and 1896, in which he set a new record for the Furthest North. He too was a creation of the press or rather of the press photographer. Like Shackleton, he was indisputably photogenic, sheer force of character burning its way down the lens. It was Nansen who had paved the way for Shackleton and his shipmates. When *Discovery* sailed down the Channel into the open sea, Nansen was still a hero of his times.

Discovery had had literally a royal send-off. She had come from Cowes, and its regatta, one of the great social events of the Season. King Edward VII himself came on board to bid farewell. He had only

Discovery *was a private expedition, although its officers were selected principally from the Navy. Shackleton, from the mercantile marine, was an exception and for the first time in his life came face to face with Navy discipline. He never felt comfortable with it. As a result he blurred the distinction between the officers and the crew, many of whom were merchant seamen like himself.*

recently ascended the throne. Shackleton was thus, appropriately, sailing out at the very start of the Edwardian era, whose short, charged span was a reflection of himself. What the King – and his subjects – thirsted for were displays of heroic endeavour. Shackleton was only too willing to oblige.

The Captain of *Discovery*, and the head of the expedition, was a certain naval officer called Robert Falcon Scott. He was an officer in the Royal Navy, newly promoted to Commander. At one level, Shackleton and he were diametric opposites. Scott was dull, uncertain, snobbish, morose and, as he quickly showed, a bit of a bully, with an aberration in his naval career hinting at unsuitability for command. Shackleton, on the other hand, was classless, forceful, engaging, cheerful and considerate to his shipmates, and his seagoing record would bear the closest inspection. But in other ways, Shackleton and Scott were mirror images of each other. Both were consumed by ambition. Each was an adventurer. That they had embarked on polar exploration was a matter of chance; they would have impartially seized any other opportunity to get on. What they also had in common was a colossal ignorance of their chosen field. That was, however, simply a manifestation of the amateur ideal. Experts need not apply.

This ideal was embodied in Sir Clements Markham, who united in his person both the originator of the expedition and its evil genius. Sir Clements was the wily President of the Royal Geographical Society. For sixteen years, he had pursued a crusade and fought official indifference to raise funds and promote the undertaking. Eventually he extracted from the Government a grant to match the private contributions. He even managed to have *Discovery* specially built. Coming from a yard in Dundee, she was the last big wooden ship to be constructed in the British Isles.

Sir Clements dominated the venture, imposing his ideas. He saw himself as the arbiter of all things polar. He wanted a naval expedition, to continue a tradition in which the Navy practically monopolised British polar exploration. After various disasters, however, the Admiralty was no longer willing, so Sir Clements had to make do with a civilian enterprise staffed by mostly naval men.

Discovery was a strange hybrid – a merchant vessel run as a warship. Shackleton was one of two merchant officers on board. The other was Albert Armitage, from the P&O line. To maintain the Naval pretence, they were thinly disguised with commissions in the Royal Naval Reserve: Shackleton as Sub-

Lieutenant and Armitage as Lieutenant. Armitage was second in command of the expedition; Shackleton mustered, in naval parlance, as Third Lieutenant, the junior officer of *Discovery*.

Scott was Sir Clements Markham's personal nominee. He had in fact been taken by Sir Clements to visit Nansen in Norway on what, among polar explorers, had become an almost obligatory pilgrimage. To both Scott and Sir Clements, it was a largely formal gesture. Ostensibly seeking advice, they ignored most of what Nansen had to say.

Of the nearly fifty men who started out on *Discovery*, most, including the Commander, had hardly even seen snow. To Sir Clements, that was not a drawback but a virtue. He saw the expedition as a means of rescuing the Navy from the decadence of prolonged peace by using the perils of the polar regions as a surrogate for war, and hence an opportunity for heroism. He deprecated experience but glorified improvisation and especially suffering as morally beneficial. He was, however, forced to accept three men who had been to the polar regions.

One was Armitage, another, Reginald Koettlitz, a doctor. Both had been to Franz Josef Land in the Arctic on a private expedition financed by Alfred Harmsworth – later Lord Northcliffe – the press magnate. Harmsworth also gave money to the *Discovery* expedition, but made the appointment of the two men a condition. The third man of experience was an Australian physicist, Louis Bernacchi, who had been on the first expedition to winter on the Antarctic continent under the Norwegian explorer, Carsten Borchgrevink. Bernacchi was on board *Discovery* because the expedition wanted a physicist, and he was the only one available. All three, like Shackleton, were under a disadvantage. They were civilian interlopers in a predominantly naval crew. Shackleton stood out most. He was not quite like an ordinary merchant officer, and a bit of a puzzle from the start. He was, however, much respected for his seamanship, including his training in sail.

That stood him in good stead, for though powered by steam, *Discovery* was also a sailing ship, a necessity because she was headed for waters far from bunkering stations. She had a reinforced wooden hull, because that was the only construction then known that could safely grapple with the ice. Unfortunately, because of official meddling in the design, she was slow, clumsy, her barque rig ill

View of Discovery *with Mount Erebus in the background. Mount Erebus was the active one of a pair of volcanoes on Ross Island, the second being named Mount Terror. It was discovered in 1841 by the British explorer Sir James Clark Ross, who named it after his ship. Mount Erebus became a familiar landmark to all the British expeditions.*

conceived and in general a bad sea boat. Even Shackleton had a hard time handling this sluggish, unresponsive vessel. At any rate, one way or another, she reached the Southern Ocean by way of New Zealand and, on 2 January 1902, after a not-too-happy voyage of five months, crossed the Antarctic Circle.

That afternoon, Shackleton saw his first southern iceberg, gleaming, sinister and flat-topped, outlier of the continent beyond. Next day, *Discovery* found the pack ice, a floating, tinted white plain, patterned by a latticework of cracks, stretching to the horizon, with the distant rumble of floe against floe, while in the sky above was the characteristic glint. *Discovery* plunged into this unfamiliar world, and after four days ran into the open Ross Sea. This had been discovered sixty years before by Admiral Sir James Clark Ross, one of the great polar explorers. *Discovery* now followed in his wake.

It was on 9 January 1902 that Shackleton first landed in Antarctica. He was on a lifeboat sent ashore at the first landfall at Cape Adare, at the entrance to the Ross Sea. The purpose was to leave a message for a relief ship. This was where Borchgrevink had become the first to winter on the Antarctic mainland. From that historic site, *Discovery* coasted down South Victoria Land, and then eastwards along the front of what was then the Ross Ice Barrier, but is known as the Ross Ice Shelf today. Shackleton was among a group on deck who sighted new land, dubbed 'King Edward VII Land' – now the King Edward VII Peninsula – which marked the eastern extremity of the ice shelf.

Soon after, he did another piece of pioneering. *Discovery* now doubled back on her tracks to the west. At a certain inlet, she put in, and it was decided amongst other things to send up a balloon specially brought for reconnaissance. Scott made the first ascent, Shackleton the second. It was Shackleton, however, who had a camera, and took the first aerial photographs in Antarctica.

Meanwhile Scott, a fair exponent of the British official's mania for secrecy, had finally revealed his plans: *Discovery* was going to winter in the ice. Shackleton at least was relieved. He had feared that the ship would be sent back to New Zealand for the winter, and that he would be on board. *Discovery* sailed on until she reached McMurdo Sound, off Ross Island, under the twin volcanoes of Terror and Erebus; the one extinct, the other steaming but quiescent. There, Scott decided to make his base. The following summer, as he had announced, he was going to make an attempt on the Pole.

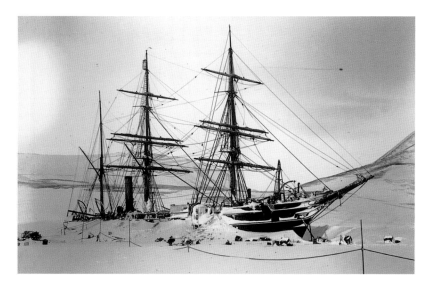

Discovery *in Winter Quarters, with Observation Hill in the background. The decision to overwinter in the south was a surprise to many of the crew, who had been expecting to return to civilisation. However, the ship became trapped between the pack ice and the shore and by the end of February 1902* Discovery *and her crew had no choice but to spend the winter in the ice at 77°50'.*

On 19 February 1902 Shackleton, in the company of Wilson and Ferrar, made his first Antarctic journey. They headed southwest towards an unnamed rock formation which was later christened White Island. On this brief expedition, Shackleton pitched a tent, encountered a blizzard and glimpsed the 'road to the South Pole' – all for the first time.

So *Discovery* was frozen in as the ice enveloped the sound, and her company, pleased or not, settled in for the winter. To a certain extent, Shackleton suffered from the antagonism between Navy and mercantile marine. With his forceful personality, he did not entirely please the naval officers on board, Lieutenants Charles Royds and, the ship's engineer, Reginald Skelton. Friendly nonetheless to all, Shackleton chose as his particular companion, however, Edward Wilson, one of the two medical men on the expedition.

A civilian rather than a naval man, Wilson combined within himself the attributes of both doctor and priest, attracting the not wholly welcome confidences of his fellows. He was obliged to listen while Shackleton, a poetry lover and indeed a would-be poet, declaimed the more florid stanzas of Browning. Overwhelmed by Shackleton, Wilson in his turn overwhelmed Scott, exerting a particular moral power. The chain of influence paid off. On 13 June 1902 Scott, secretly prompted by Wilson, told Shackleton that he had chosen him to join the two of them during the southern summer on the attempt to reach the Pole. Shackleton was overjoyed. It was the outcome he ardently desired – and it was also a logical one, for he had already had his initiation.

Soon after arriving at McMurdo Sound, Scott had sent him out to reconnoitre the start of the route. On 19 February, Shackleton started off. With him, he had two companions. Wilson was one and Hartley Ferrar, the expedition's geologist, the other. Both happened to be Cambridge graduates and beginners in snow travel, like Shackleton himself. Scott had carefully kept back with him on the ship the experienced polar travellers, Armitage, Koettlitz and Bernacchi. So too had he done with the skis and the sledge dogs that, reluctantly, he had been persuaded to take by Nansen. Shackleton led his little party into the unknown, tramping dully through the snow, hauling their own sledges.

Such was their initiation into polar travel – a case of the lame leading the blind. It was an epic of improvisation, with undertones of comedy. Nobody had pitched a tent before, much less used a Primus stove out in the field. It was the first occasion, however, on which Shackleton had been given command. In such unpromising circumstances, he came into his own. A leader was being revealed. Somehow, running the gauntlet of unfamiliar ice and snow, he got his party all the few miles to their goal, and safely back to the ship.

From left to right, Shackleton, Scott and Wilson before starting south. Shackleton set off towards the Pole with his two companions firmly believing it was within their grasp. Beyond them lay 750 miles of unknown territory. The party was described by Bernacchi as that of 'three polar knights . . . a small party but full of grit and determination'.

This was the most successful of the experimental forays, on one of which a man was killed through collective ignorance of ice. Shackleton suffered no such accidents. From the top of a protruding rock pinnacle called White Island, he looked down over the gently billowing ice stretching as far as the eye could see. In his role of precursor, he had discovered the road to the South. Now, almost nine months later, on 2 November, he finally set off on that same road in earnest, together with Scott and Wilson – and thought he would be the victor as well.

This journey, alas, was doomed before it began. Little had been done since landing to repair the ignorance of ice and snow. A large body of published material on snow travel existed, from the tribes of Siberia, Greenland and North America, to the European and American Arctic explorers. It was wilfully ignored. So too was the practical knowledge, closer to home, of the three members of the expedition with polar experience. Shackleton, Scott and Wilson were condemned to learning as they went along. They were using dogs to pull their sledges, but understood the technique not at all, so it turned into a bitter struggle of tragedy and farce, the animals being incompetently butchered as they failed. Nobody knew how to use skis, so Scott ordained that they be dragged uselessly, as dead weight on the sledges. The men toiled for a derisory few miles a day. It soon became apparent that the Pole was out of reach, so that what remained was a record for the Furthest South, which meant no more than knowing when to turn back.

But that itself involved a conflict among the ill-assorted trio, riddled from the start with underlying strain. Scott obstinately wanted to blunder on ahead, even when scurvy appeared. He did not understand that he had overrun his supplies and he was in an irrational state of mind. It was Wilson who persuaded him to turn. They finally did so on New Year's Eve. Shackleton had wanted to turn back long before. Their record was 82°17' South. Although they had advanced 240 miles further than anyone before, they all agreed that the final result was not particularly impressive. Shackleton had no regrets. Unlike the others, with their half-formed yearnings of martyrdom, he only wanted to get back alive.

The retreat turned into a desperate plodding race against extinction in the snows. In the process the tensions between Shackleton and Scott grew, and there was a quarrel along the way. It was precipitated by an outburst of uncontrollable temper in Scott. Then Shackleton fell ill. All three men were in the grip

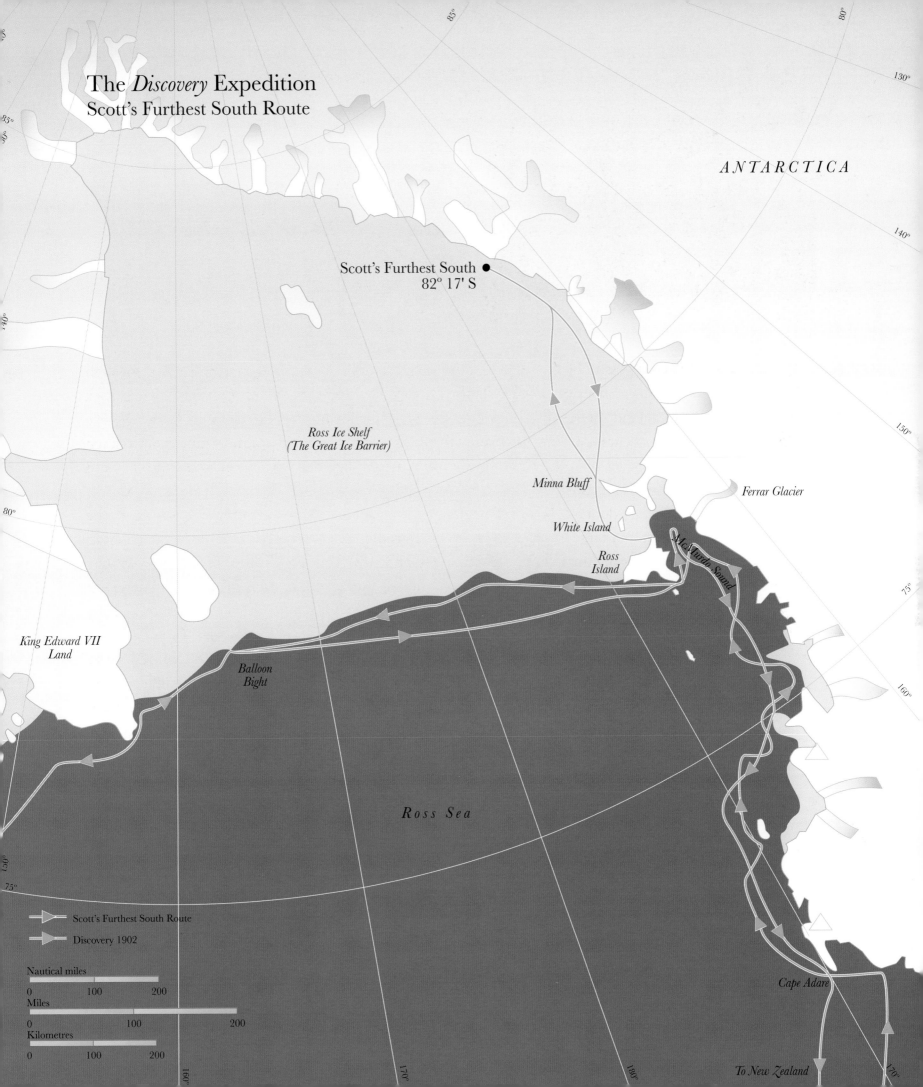

The *Discovery* Expedition
Scott's Furthest South Route

ANTARCTICA

Scott's Furthest South ●
82° 17' S

Ross Ice Shelf
(The Great Ice Barrier)

Minna Bluff

Ferrar Glacier

White Island

McMurdo Sound

Ross
Island

King Edward VII
Land

Balloon
Bight

Ross Sea

Cape Adare

Scott's Furthest South Route

Discovery 1902

Nautical miles

| 0 | 100 | 200 |

Miles

| 0 | 100 | 200 |

Kilometres

| 0 | 100 | 200 |

To New Zealand

'Alone! Alone, all, all alone'
Alone on a wide wide sea
And never a saint took pity on
The in men Agony

Coleridge

Ancient Mariner

Shackleton, Scott and Wilson on arrival at Discovery *after the arduous Southern Sledge Journey. The three exhausted men were met some five miles from the ship by Bernacchi and Skelton, the first humans they had seen in nearly three months. The quotation, in Shackleton's hand, is from Coleridge's 'Ancient Mariner'. However, it was in fact Tennyson's 'Ulysses' that 'kept running through [Shackleton's] head' during the journey.*

Cheering the relief ship. Ten days before Shackleton, Scott and Wilson returned to Discovery, *the relief ship* Morning *had appeared on the horizon. The expedition members had not seen a fresh face or had contact with the world beyond the ice in over a year. This image captures that joy at the thought of a return to civilisation.*

of scurvy – its cause, an acute lack of vitamin C, then unknown. Shackleton, however, was also suffering from some indefinable ailment connected with heart and lungs. In great distress, wheezing and coughing up blood, he somehow struggled on. Skis were his salvation. Two pairs had been jettisoned to reduce weight. One had been kept for emergencies. To save his strength, Shackleton put them on and floated on the snow, while his companions stubbornly floundered on. The dogs had all been killed as useless, so it was man-hauling all the way.

On 3 February 1903, after a journey of heroic suffering, with failing supplies and no margin of safety, the three men returned to *Discovery*. During the last day or two, Shackleton had mysteriously recovered, and seemed stronger than his companions. Like them he had shown willpower, but also something else.

At McMurdo Sound, there was a relief ship, *Morning*. *Discovery* was still frozen in, and would remain so for another year. Scott took the opportunity to send Shackleton home, ostensibly on the grounds of ill health, but really in consequence of their quarrel on the Southern Journey. They had in fact a fundamental incompatibility. Besides their other differences, Scott was jealous and dependent on a hierarchy for command, while Shackleton drew on his inherent powers. Furthermore, Shackleton, the stronger character, was a threat to Scott's authority. Almost from the start, Shackleton had seized the psychological leadership and for that he now had to pay. On 1 March 1903, he unwillingly trudged over the ice separating *Discovery* from open water and embarked on *Morning*.

Many on board *Discovery* were now sorry to see him go: Armitage for one, but also Michael Barne, one of his lieutenants. Shackleton had turned out to be an entertaining messmate. He had also made his mark among the ratings. In a moving gesture, they spontaneously cheered him in farewell. Shackleton had the common touch. As he watched what had seemed the Promised Land recede, he burst into tears. He was also nursing a bitter resentment. At the southernmost camp, Scott and Wilson had walked on alone, leaving him behind on guard, as they said. He could therefore only claim 82°15' or so, and was therefore not entitled fully to share the record for the Furthest South. He was sailing away with a complicated mixture of disappointment, frustration and desire for revenge. It was a lethal cocktail of emotion.

Madeira — Costumes populares

No. 66 Verlag von Alberto Nobre, Hamburg

on: We have a good pass and Yours

This postcard was sent by Shackleton
to his sister Amy on 18 August 1901 from
Funchal, the first port of call on *Discovery*'s
outward journey. Communication with
home became increasingly important as the
ship sailed further south. When they arrived
in New Zealand Shackleton disembarked
immediately and woke the postmaster,
demanding the post for the ship. While
Shackleton was waiting for news from
Emily, he was aware that his friend Wilson
would be anxious to hear from his wife,
whom he had married only two weeks
before sailing with *Discovery*.

1 A crowd of several thousand well-wishers gathered on Christmas Eve 1901 to see Scott and his men depart from Lyttelton harbour, New Zealand. As *Discovery* sailed out of the harbour she was still 1,100 miles from the Antarctic Circle.

2 Improvised studding sails were necessary, since 'the ship steered badly, there being too much sail aft and not enough forward'. Shackleton feared that this problem, already noted in the early stages of the voyage, would become a much more serious matter. *Discovery* was headed for some of the roughest seas on the planet.

1

1 Deep-sea sound at 1,500 fathoms (9,000 feet deep) on the journey south. Oceanography was part of *Discovery*'s work and this photograph may have been taken whilst sounding in the Southern Ocean between Cape Town and New Zealand.

2 Two members of the crew struggling with an albatross on deck. Sailors believed that if an albatross landed aboard ship it was a bad omen since the souls of dead sailors were preserved in the birds.

1 On 2 January 1902 Shackleton saw his first
  iceberg. These great islands of ice, some
  the size of counties, pirouetted slowly in
  a mysterious dance around one another.
  Suddenly the expedition had entered a new
  world, one of snow and ice, sea and sky –
  immense, desolate and beautiful.
  Expressions of awe and wonder are
  recorded in the men's diaries.

2 Tabular Iceberg, 260 feet high, was a
  particularly impressive berg which the
  expedition encountered in February 1902.

3 Calved from great glaciers, the icebergs
  were sculpted and shaped by the winds
  and waves. With up to four fifths of their
  mysterious forms hidden below the water,
  they represented a menacing presence for
  the ships.

1 *Discovery*'s first landing on the ice barrier was in the Bay of Whales, where they anchored and set up the reconnaissance balloon, 'Eva'. Although Shackleton had undergone a few days training in Aldershot and felt himself to be well qualified to fly the balloon, it was Scott who insisted on making the maiden flight on 4 February 1902.

2, 3 Inflating the balloon, photographed by Shackleton. The balloon was made of cow gut and had to be handled with great care, as did the hydrogen that they had brought with them in cylinders.

1 Shackleton was second up and recorded
with some private satisfaction that he had
succeeded in going up to 650 feet, higher
than Scott. He took this photograph from
400 feet, showing below him *Discovery* tied
to the Barrier side in the Inlet and the dark
shadow of the balloon on the Barrier
surface. Taken on 4 February 1902, this was
the first aerial photograph of the Antarctic.

2 When Shackleton descended he handed
over to Wilson, who refused to get into the
basket, deeming it to be perfect madness.
They then discovered that the balloon had a
leaky valve; had that valve been used, the
balloon and its pilot would have fallen to
earth like a stone. The balloon was packed
away never to be used again, and that day
became known as 'Balloon Bight'.

1 Bird's-eye view of Winter Quarters. Shortly
  after Balloon Bight, *Discovery* became
  trapped between the pack ice and land.
  There was no choice but to overwinter in
  Antarctica. There she remained from
  February 1902 to February 1904.

2 Scott had brought with him a portable hut,
  which he ordered to be erected on the ice. It
  was used as a store. The hut lent its name to
  the promontory on which it stood on Ross
  Island, which became known as Hut Point.

3 Moonlight view of *Discovery* in Winter
  Quarters, May 1902, starboard bow. The
  Antarctic winter was long and although
  there was a slight glow on the horizon
  towards midday, the darkness oppressed the
  men. Cramped aboard, they remained as
  active as possible to keep up morale.

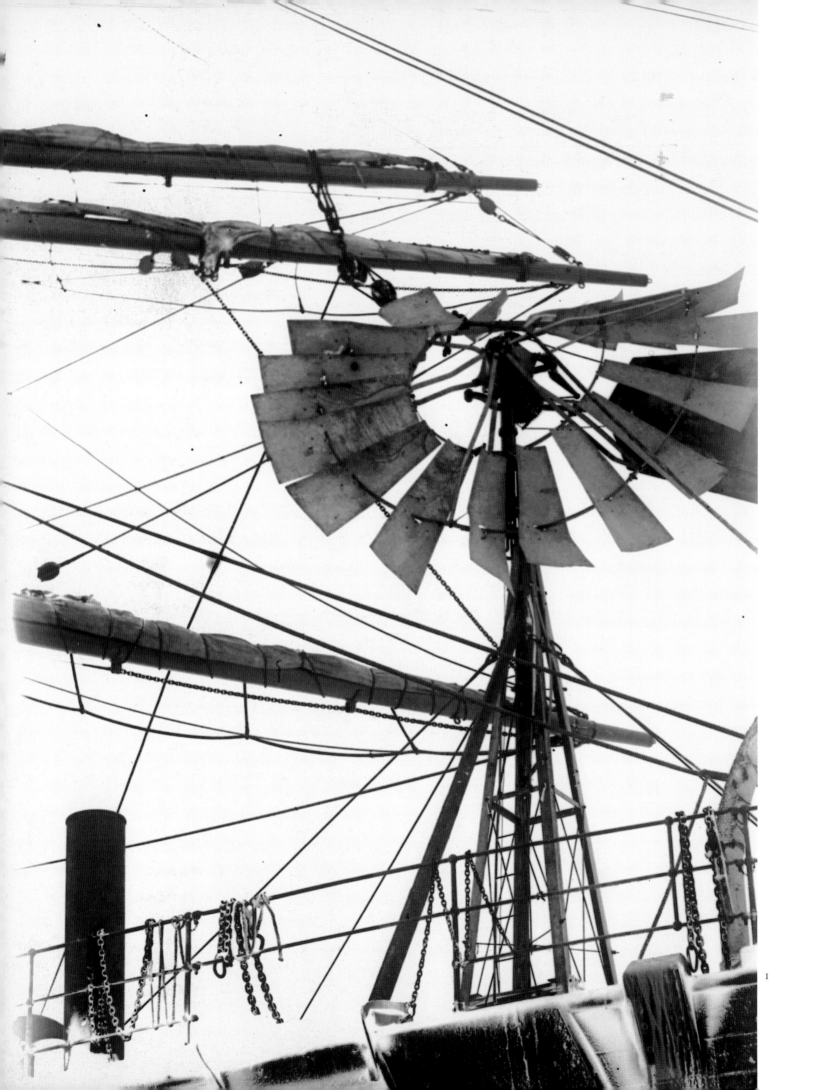

2

1 Nothing could speak more eloquently of the forces of nature than this image of the damaged windmill after the gale of 13 April 1902. The wind raged in furious gusts around the ship until eventually the storm blew itself out and the crew could survey the damage.

2 Snowfall is as rare in Antarctica as rain in the Sahara. However, when there is a gale, snow is whipped up and deposited in drifts in new places. The result of the first gale in April 1902 was that a great amount of snow had built up against the side of the ship and this had to be dug out by the men.

3 One of the features of the expedition was the scientific work that Scott encouraged. He required a meteorological survey to be set up on top of what came to be called Crater Hill. For Shackleton it provided an excuse to take some much-needed exercise and to escape from the oppressive atmosphere aboard the ship.

3

I

1 The inside of the Hut, 26 May 1902, showing a variety of stored materials and equipment, including the pendulum apparatus on a brick pedestal, snow shoes on the wall and boxes of biscuits, which were used for the sledging journey.
2 The first crop of mustard and cress grown on Antarctic soil.
3 In addition to the Hut, there was also a general store, where tinned food was kept. Nutrition as a science was in its infancy and Scott and the Navy believed that dried and tinned food would be the best for their men. Scott was dismissive of Shackleton's claim that fresh meat was healthier.

2

3

1 One of the daily tasks for all the Antarctic
  expeditions was the collection of ice for
  drinking water. It was laborious work but
  necessary. Water was also required for
  cooking, washing and cleaning the ship, as
  well as for the dogs.
2, 3 The ice had to be cut into blocks and
  dragged on sledges to the ship for melting. It
  was known as 'watering the ship' and here it
  is being carried out by the crew. Over the
  period of two years several tons of ice were
  melted to keep the expedition alive.

123

1 Scott was keen to set fish traps if possible but this involved blowing a hole in the ice and to this end the Torpedo men, Arthur Pilbeam and Thomas Kennar, were enlisted to help. Here they are photographed fitting detonators to the gun cotton charges.
2 It was Scott himself who daringly placed the fuse for exploding the ice.
3 After the fuse was lit the men ran away as fast as they could before the explosion.
4 The gun-cotton explosion boomed spectacularly, sending a jet of ice, mud and water tens of feet into the air.

3

4

1 Penguins, a potent symbol of Antarctica, were extensively studied during the *Discovery* expedition. Adélie penguins, as seen here, were stouter and more comical than the Emperor penguins, which stood over three feet tall.

2 Royd is shown here as if talking to the penguin. The penguins encountered by the early British expeditions were as interested in human beings as vice versa. Apparently unafraid, they made visits to inspect the ships and huts.

3 An Adélie penguin examining Lyle's golden syrup tins.

4 Young Emperor penguins. Wilson was particularly fascinated by the life-cycle of Emperor penguins at the Cape Crozier Rookery at the commencement of the Great Barrier, and he later published the results of his research.

3

Overleaf: The Emperor is the most majestic
and impressive of all penguins. The males
overwinter on the ice, hundreds of miles
from the sea, protecting the females' eggs,
while the females winter out at sea,
returning sleek and fat to relieve their
partners in the Antarctic spring.

4

2

1

1 Here penguins are being weighed. Penguins provided not only scientific interest and entertainment for the men, they were also a vital source of fresh meat, supplementing the diet of seal meat as well as providing food for the sledge dogs.

2 Shackleton at Cape Adare. Unlike Scott, who hated to see anything killed, Shackleton was quite happy to go out hunting for seal and penguin. He relished any opportunity to get away from the ship and would often be found leading a sealing party or walking down to the rifle range for target practice.

1 One of the great scourges of ocean travel was scurvy. At the time the cause was unknown, but Shackleton knew intuitively that scurvy had something to do with diet and he insisted that the men should eat fresh meat wherever possible. So insistent was he that he set out with a party of hunters to kill seals to provide fresh food.

2 Royds and Feather stand over their kill – two crab-eating seals. Shackleton demanded that the cook prepare seal meat for the men. However, it was some time before the men below decks would agree to eat it since the chef, in the first instance, made it so unpalatable.

3 Hauling a slaughtered seal back to the ship. Scott finally backed Shackleton, ordering the cook to prepare the meat in a way that would please the men.

3

I

1 The *Discovery* is loaded with ice, while seal meat hangs from her rigging. Shackleton not only convinced Scott that seal and penguin meat should be prepared for the men for food, but also succeeded in killing for storage, so that when the animals left the ice there would be sufficient reserves. The meat was hung in the rigging, where it was effectively freeze-dried until required.

2 Once the light had returned after the long winter months, the men made forays in pairs or larger groups for exercise. One of the extraordinary phenomena they encountered were the ridges that appeared sporadically in the ice. Skelton and a companion had skied over to this ridge in Seal Bay, which they were using as a slide. Note their single ski stick in the foreground.

I

1 Skelton with a half-plate camera, photographed by Shackleton in September 1902. There was no official photographer on the *Discovery* expedition but the ship's engineer, Lieutenant Reginald Skelton, was a competent photographer and many of the *Nimrod* images in the book come from his collection.

2 Skelton travelling on skis, photographed by Shackleton. Long recognised by the Norwegians, amongst other Polar travellers, as the most efficient, not to say enjoyable, way of travelling across snow, skiing was not rated by Scott's men. Very late in the day he ordered his men to learn to ski, but, with no proper instruction, they failed miserably, forgoing this mode of transport and marching on foot instead.

2

1 Shackleton's 'rum idea' was a little sledge on wheels, which he believed would be efficient for use on the ice. It was not used for the Southern Journey, as the wheels soon became clogged with snow when any weight was placed upon it.

2 A group of officers on the floe alongside *Discovery* make their first attempts at skiing. The skis, made of wood, had no edges and were fastened at the toe only, and there was just one pole, rather than the two used today. Instead of adopting the seemingly effortless Norwegian style of skiing, the British plodded on their skis, using them more like snow shoes. They were disappointed in the result and complained bitterly about falling over regularly.

Overleaf: The Southern Depot Sledge Party comprised over a dozen men. They would lay depots for Scott, Shackleton and Wilson for their return journey from the South. Their clothing presented them with real problems – the Burberry windproof jackets lacked fixed hoods, were too tight and did not breathe, so that the men sweated whilst on the move and then froze when they stood still.

2

1

2

1 Scott's sledging journey with Barne and
Shackleton. The Southern Journey had two
sledges, each weighing one and a half tons.
One sledge had a meter – in the form of a
wheel – attached to it, which allowed the
team to clock their mileage both for safety
reasons and for the record.

2 Harnessing dogs for the Southern Sledge
Party. It was a last-minute decision to take
the dogs south. None of the men was
trained in dog handling, and as a result the
dogs performed poorly for them. In the end,
all the dogs died on the Southern Journey,
of either exhaustion or food poisoning.

5

1, 2, 3, 4 At the beginning of December Shackleton observed to the west a mountain range, which was in fact part of the Transantarctic Mountains, one end of which had been discovered by Sir James Clark Ross in 1841 and named the Admiralty Range. This colossal curve of

mountains, peak after peak, stretched as far as the eye could see. Wilson recorded in his diary how very small and insignificant he felt, a mere speck in the middle of an enormous plain.

5 Looking south along a movement chasm on the Great Ice Barrier, photographed by

Shackleton, 15 December 1902. The weather had been fickle, with swirling mists obscuring their view, but on this day the mist lifted, making their progress slightly easier. Shackleton's health, however, was giving cause for concern.

'How splendid the Western mountains looked today! Tongue or pen or pencil would sadly fail were they to attempt to describe the magic of the colouring and later on the afternoon the very clouds light and fleecy were of rainbow hue. Iridescent and opaline in their many tints. Days like these stand out amongst the grey ones that are so common here. The sunset was a poem. The change of twilight into night, which was lighted by the crescent moon, was weirdly beautiful, for the cliffs of white gave no part of their colour away and the rocks beside them did not part with their blackness so that it was a curious effect of the deepening shadow over these contrasts.'

From Shackleton's diary, 10 September 1902

1

2

1 Christmas Day 1902: Wilson recognised that the outbreak of scurvy had put an end to their hopes of reaching the South Pole. Scott was adamant that they should continue but after a heated debate agreed to turn back on 28 December.

2 'New Lands, Southern Sledge Journey, 28 December 1902' was sketched by Wilson. This was the day set by Scott on Christmas Day for turning back, but when the time came, convinced that his scurvy was on the mend and determined to reach

the pressure ridges to the south of their current position, he could not bring himself to do it. Two days later, in a whiteout, the men finally turned.

'It is settled for our furthest South to be on 28th [December] then we go into the land. Medical examtn shews Captain and I to be inclined to scurvy . . . What a Christmas baking hot. It must have been so different at home.'

From Shackleton's diary, Christmas Day 1902

'. . . to-night Wilson told me that Shackleton has decidedly angry-looking gums [scurvy], and that for some time they have been slowly but surely getting worse. He says there is nothing yet to be alarmed at, but he now thought it serious enough to tell me in view of our future plans . . . it is a matter which must be thought out. Certainly this is a black night, but things must look blacker yet before we decide to turn.'

From Scott's book of the expedition, published in 1905 as *The Voyage of the Discovery*. Purporting to quote his diary, but really elaborating afterwards, 21 December 1902

1

1 Southern Sledge Party on the Great Ice Barrier, 24 January 1903. A month into their return journey Shackleton took this photograph. While all three men were suffering from scurvy, Shackleton was also blighted with severe chest pains and a shortness of breath.

2 Return of Captain Scott and the Southern Sledge Party with annotations. The men were met some five miles from the ship by Bernacchi and Skelton, who found them weak and exhausted. Skelton remarked that where it had seemed an enormous effort for Scott and Wilson to pull the sledge, for him and his fit companion it was almost no effort. Such was the state of deterioration. And Shackleton was weaker still. Sheer willpower, it seemed, had kept him going.

Return of the Southern
Sledge-party.
Feb. 2. 1903.

Capt. Scott

E. a. Wilson.

Cross.

Skelton

Bernacchi

Armitage.

2

'A beautiful day, but a sad one indeed for me . . . I cannot write much about it . . . Ah, it is hard to have to leave before the work is over and especially to leave those who will have to stay down here in the cold dark days for there seems to my mind but little chance of the old ship [*Discovery*] going out.'

From Shackleton's diary, when leaving in the relief ship *Morning* on being invalided home, 28 February 1903

1 Scott decided that Shackleton was too ill to remain with *Discovery*, which was firmly frozen into the ice and would be forced to spend another winter in McMurdo Sound. He was therefore more or less ordered by Scott to return with *Morning* whilst the rest of the men stayed with *Discovery* for a further winter. It was a moment of bitter disappointment for Shackleton.

2 The company of *Discovery* after their return to London in November 1904. Shackleton joined them for the photograph, but he had not forgiven Scott for sending him home on *Morning*. Scott went on publicly to humiliate Shackleton by telling the *Daily Mail* that he and Wilson had had to pull Shackleton on the sledge.

2

3

NIMROD AND NEAR SUCCESS ON THE POLAR PLATEAU 1907-9

Opposite: Ernest Shackleton, September 1908. He and three others had arrived within a hundred miles of the South Pole, at 87°22'. For three years Shackleton was the Edwardian hero who had been closer to the South Pole than any other.
Right: A hundred copies of Aurora Australis *were printed during the* Nimrod *expedition. They were bound with venesta boards from packing cases.*

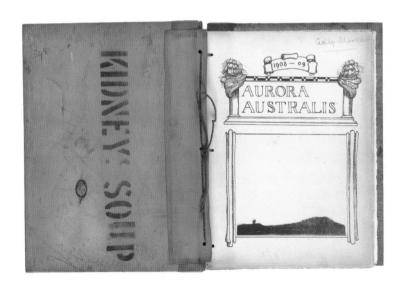

*Emily Dorman married
Ernest Shackleton on
9 April 1904 at Christchurch,
Westminster. She was thirty-
five years old, six years older
than her husband. Emily did
not espouse the current trend
for women's independence,
although, ironically, it was
her own inherited wealth that
provided a stable family income.*

In one way, however, Shackleton was more or less content. He had gone south to acquire fame, and especially fortune, to satisfy the father of the girl he wanted to marry. She was Emily Dorman, who lived in the same London suburb in which he had grown up. Her father, Charles Dorman, was a solicitor of means, who did not quite see it as the ideal match, since Emily had inherited money of her own, Shackleton had only what he earned. Mr Dorman, however, died while Shackleton was sailing to the Antarctic. Emily, long since of age, had decided to marry Shackleton but, by the custom of the times, still deferred to her menfolk. The head of the family was now her elder brother Herbert, a solicitor like his

father. He was rather easier to square. On 9 April 1904, Shackleton finally married his Emily. He had just passed his thirtieth birthday; she was six years his senior.

They set up house in Edinburgh. There, Shackleton had been appointed Secretary to the Royal Scottish Geographical Society. It was this sheen of respectability – albeit at a nugatory stipend – that overcame Herbert Dorman's reservations. Before finding the post – through the charitable jobbery of a friend – Shackleton had exploited the Antarctic to break into journalism. In a way, it had begun out there, when he edited *The South Polar Times*. This was the expedition magazine, typewritten, but somewhat less amateurish than others of its kind. However, a short stint in London on his return proved that journalism was no more an instant path to wealth and position than the mercantile marine from which he had now resigned.

Even the Royal Scottish Geographical Society was no more than a staging post. Shackleton was restless, bustling around, always impatiently looking for the next path to

On Sunday 4 August 1907 King Edward VII, Queen Alexandra and Admiral Sir John Fisher, the First Sea Lord, inspected Nimrod at Cowes. The Queen gave Shackleton a flag to plant at the South Pole and the King conferred on him the Royal Victorian Order. A grander send-off could hardly have been possible.

success. At least when Scott returned from the Antarctic in 1904, after a second, undistinguished season in the ice, the record for the Furthest South remained untouched. He had, however, been promoted to Captain – admittedly through family influence – and was a kind of authorised hero, while Shackleton remained a nobody.

Perhaps that is why Shackleton henceforth took on occasion to calling himself 'Lieutenant', on the strength of his commission in the Royal Naval Reserve, although he had actually resigned just before his marriage. There was even an unsuccessful attempt by friendly officers to get him a regular commission in the Navy itself.

Meanwhile, Shackleton tried his hand first at business, part-time, and then at politics. He was asked to stand as a Conservative and Unionist candidate for Dundee. However, he failed to appreciate the fact that he was no more than a makeweight in a hopeless seat. At the general election of 1906, he duly lost. As another quick path to success, politics had failed, and Shackleton moved on. Yet he was not exactly a drifter. He had a sense of hidden powers within himself, which he was struggling to release.

At one point, Shackleton had made the acquaintance of William Beardmore, a prominent Clydeside industrialist. Beardmore, part struck, part amused by Shackleton's very own blend of blarney, vaunting ambition and overwhelming personality, had promised him a job in case he failed to win a parliamentary seat. That undertaking Beardmore now honoured and, in the spring of 1906, Shackleton found himself with regular employment in what we would now call public relations. After a short daydream of instant riches yet

again, Shackleton cast about for a more alluring prospect and turned once more to the Antarctic. Of official support there was scant hope, so he resorted to private patronage instead. He went to Beardmore, who, in February 1907, agreed to back an attempt on the South Pole. Earth-bound businessman as he was, Beardmore had long since grasped that Shackleton was not someone who could easily settle down. An Antarctic expedition was an honourable pretext to send him on his way. But prudently Beardmore had not handed over any money. Instead he guaranteed a loan of £7,000 at the bank. It was not much, but for Shackleton it was enough.

Before going to work for Beardmore, Shackleton, in another abortive chapter in his quest for wealth, had become involved in some doubtful promotions on the London stock exchange. His younger brother, Frank, was also concerned. By playing on those contacts, especially Frank, Shackleton managed to raise most of the extra money, or at least the credit, he required.

It was a considerable achievement. With no means of his own and, not to put too fine a point on it, living off his wife, Shackleton had somehow managed to organise an expedition. Behind the façade of empty talk, he was proving to be the kind of man who, mysteriously, could make things happen. As his expedition ship, he bought an old weatherworn, ice-scarred sealer of some 300 tons called *Nimrod*. She came from Newfoundland, but had been built in Dundee, the last home of wooden ships.

With an unfolding talent for contacts in high places, Shackleton managed to engineer a royal send-off. At the last moment, like *Discovery* before her, *Nimrod* was ordered to Cowes during the regatta and, as on that occasion, King Edward VII came on board to inspect the ship. Behind his reputation of rake and *bon vivant*, the King was very well informed and knew much about the expedition. He evidently admired this example of private enterprise, and especially the buccaneering figure of its Commander. On 5 August 1907, *Nimrod* headed into the Channel. It was a bare seven months since the start of the expedition – a whirlwind of preparation.

Shackleton himself did not actually leave for another three months, finally departing by mail ship at the end of October. This gave him much needed extra time for business and domestic affairs. When he left, despite all kinds of pressure, it was with deep satisfaction. On *Nimrod*, the King had presented

Shackleton with the Royal Victorian Order, explicitly because he had done so to Scott. But in certain respects Shackleton had outdone Scott: *Discovery* had merely been present at a regatta, while *Nimrod* was commanded to a naval review as well – that of the Home Fleet, the most powerful naval force on earth. What is more, Queen Alexandra, King Edward's consort, had presented Shackleton with a flag to plant, as she, and others, expected, at the very South Pole itself. This was the first action of its kind. At every turn, Shackleton had been comparing himself with Scott. It was wounded pride and hunger for revenge that, in the last resort, had sent *Nimrod* on her way.

This was not only due to Shackleton's invaliding home from *Discovery*. It was also caused by the airing of his ill health on the Southern Journey in Scott's book on the expedition, published in 1905 as *The Voyage of the Discovery*. Scott blamed Shackleton for the poor Furthest South record, implying that by his weakness he alone had scurvy, when all three, as Scott well knew, had contracted the disease. Other examples of fraudulence, coupled with a vein of hubris, were only further goads.

In fact, towards the end of 1905, Shackleton had already made his first, optimistic attempt to organise an Antarctic expedition. What really nourished his loathing for Scott was that Scott had revealed a corner of the truth. Shackleton knew that all was not well with him. He felt somehow that time was running out. He wanted to succeed before it was too late.

At the beginning of December, after a passage of a month, Shackleton arrived in Adelaide. The expedition was in fact not yet secure. His finances were in disarray. He still needed several thousand pounds. The Australian government stepped into the breach with a grant of £5,000 – the first public help he had received. At home, he had been snubbed by the Establishment, especially the upholders of institutionalised mediocrity in the Royal Geographical Society. The qualities that aroused such antagonism, truculent self-reliance, independence and such a disregard for authority appealed to the young Australian nation. Even in the heyday of Empire, England, the mother country, was equated with stuffiness. The Australians appreciated a trier. Before he had even started, Shackleton was adopted as a local hero, and basked in the unaccustomed warmth.

He had the same reception in New Zealand, where he now went to join *Nimrod*. The Government

there gave him another £1,000. Even this, together with a private gift of £500, did not balance the books, but at least it enabled him to sail as intended from Lyttelton, the closest practicable port to the Antarctic, on New Year's Day 1908. As she cleared land, *Nimrod* looked vaguely like a pirate ship. That, in essence, is what she was.

Behind him, Shackleton had left a trail of confusion. It was not only money. He had temporarily abandoned his wife to look after two children, one of them a young baby. After less than three years of marriage, Emily had realised that domesticity, after all, would not satisfy her husband. She was prematurely sinking into a mood of resignation. Shackleton had already succumbed to an entanglement of sorts with Beardmore's wife Elspeth, and at least a passionate flirtation with someone else on the voyage out to Australia. But once *Nimrod* had put the coast astern, Shackleton shed the behaviour of a man out of his element ashore, and assumed the more agreeable personality of his seagoing self. There were, however, still difficulties ahead.

An auxiliary barquentine, with too little sail, low, dark and underpowered, *Nimrod* wallowed in the southern waves. At the last moment, Shackleton realised, that unaided, he could not make his landfall in time. Nor could *Nimrod* carry enough coal. So the New Zealand authorities provided him with a tow, in the shape of a tramp steamer called *Koonya*. Linked by a cable, the two vessels somehow forced their way through the violent rollers of an incessant, nightmarish storm, green seas raking *Nimrod* from stem to stern. After a fortnight, a white band of what appeared to be the pack ice hove into sight. *Koonya*, being made of iron, could not cope with ice, and turned back. At this severing of the last link with civilisation, Shackleton noticeably relaxed. But quite at ease he was not.

The white line proved to be not the expected pack ice, but a freakish belt of icebergs. The probable cause soon appeared. After a few days, *Nimrod*, her stovepipe funnel belching thick smoke, ran out into the open Ross Sea and headed for Balloon Bight on the Barrier, which Shackleton had seen with his own eyes on *Discovery* a bare six years before. The inlet had disappeared. The gloomy Barrier front had calved, sending it out to sea, and broken back to form a new bay, with whales spouting from the dark swell. On this account, the new feature was dubbed the 'Bay of Whales', and as such passed into history.

An intricate web of circumstance had sent Shackleton to the Bay of Whales, instead of the more familiar McMurdo Sound. To begin with, Albert Armitage, from *Discovery*, had suggested it as a preferable base, because it was closer to the Pole. What was really hounding Shackleton, however, was the sullen demon he saw in Scott. When Scott heard of Shackleton's intentions, he erupted in a fury fuelled by what he saw was his prescriptive right. He too wanted to return and conquer the Pole, and the whole Ross Sea he saw as his domain. He demanded that Shackleton keep out. Through the mediation of Wilson, he finally agreed that Shackleton could use the Ross Sea, but only to the east of 170° West longitude. To avoid a public quarrel and a threat to the whole expedition, Shackleton signed an undertaking to that effect.

The cataclysmic break up of the ice front decided Shackleton against ever wintering on the Barrier. After an abortive attempt to land on King Edward VII Land, he decided, after all, to turn on his tracks and make for McMurdo Sound. He did so, however, with a heavy heart. Though the promise extracted from him was one that Scott had no right to demand, Shackleton felt that he was nonetheless breaking his word. As *Nimrod* steamed west towards the forbidden waters of McMurdo Sound, Shackleton sensed the workings of Nemesis, which neither he nor Scott could escape.

At the end of January 1908, *Nimrod* entered McMurdo Sound, and Shackleton was reunited with scenes of ambiguous memory. After three weeks of hard work, playing cat and mouse with running surf, he had partly built his hut and established his base, not at the old *Discovery* winter quarters, but a little north at Cape Royds, under Mount Erebus. On 22 February, *Nimrod* sailed off, taking with her all outside troubles. It was with unmitigated relief that Shackleton saw her lumber over the swell among the gathering floes and fade, hull down, into the distance.

Nimrod's Journey to McMurdo Sound

ANTARCTICA

Ross Ice Shelf
(The Great Ice Barrier)

Minna Bluff

Ferrar Glacier

White Island

Ross
Island

McMurdo Sound

King Edward VII
Land

Bay of
Whales

Ross Sea

Cape Adare

Nautical miles

0   100   200

Miles

0   100   200

Kilometres

0   100   200

From New Zealand

85°

80°

130°

140°

150°

75°

160°

170°

160°

170°

180°

Shackleton had ignored advice from his Norwegian friends and elected to take horses rather than dogs to tow the sledges. Manchurian ponies were chosen for their strength and hardiness. These four – Socks, Quan, Chinaman and Grisi – were the ones chosen to make the journey to the South Pole.

Isolated from the outside world, Shackleton was now marooned on the desolate edge of Antarctica with an ill-assorted menagerie of men and beasts. The debacle of the *Discovery* expedition had left Shackleton with a mistrust of dogs, instead of doubts over their masters. Prompted by Armitage, who had seen ponies used on Franz Josef Land, he decided to take them as draught animals instead. As a result, Cape Royds witnessed the bizarre sight of eight Manchurian ponies on the shore. They were thoroughly out of place. Shaggy-haired, and adapted to a certain depth of cold, they were nonetheless herbivores. In the whole barren Antarctic continent, there was no grazing. Fodder had laboriously to be carried on an overloaded *Nimrod*. In the age of Empire, the British seemed intent on making things as uncomfortable for themselves as they possibly could.

Despite his distrust of the breed, Shackleton had abruptly taken nine sledge dogs at the last moment from New Zealand. Perhaps it was a kind of insurance. They were the descendants of animals left behind by Borchgrevink, the Norwegian Antarctic pioneer, at the beginning of the century. At any rate, the dogs were obviously at home. Being carnivores, they had all the food they could possibly want in the form of seals that ringed the land. No doubt to their utter disbelief, they were left to laze, while their masters wearily hauled sledges here and there. This the men did on foot. Shackleton had abandoned skis, despite their having probably saved his life on the previous expedition. He mistrusted them as much as he did the dogs, and for much the same reasons. That is, he blamed the tools for the workman's failings.

His companions had been chosen with equal lack of logic. No more than Scott, did Shackleton demand knowledge of ice and snow. Of the fifteen men to land, only Shackleton himself, together with two others, Ernest Joyce and Frank Wild, had polar experience, all having been together on *Discovery* – Joyce and Wild from the lower deck. In Australia, three other beginners had joined. One was an aimless, tortured, self-reviling soul called Bertram Armytage. The others were geologists: Professor Edgeworth David, Welsh-born, eloquent and persuasive, from the University of Sydney, and Douglas Mawson, from Adelaide. There was a third geologist, in the person of Raymond Priestley, a young English student seemingly plucked at random from the then University College, now the University of Bristol. It was not only the necessity of a sheen of science that persuaded Shackleton to take these men. He was a treasure

hunter at heart and, besides the riches that he expected to flow from the attainment of the Pole itself, he was hoping for gold or jewels in Antarctica. Naturally he needed geologists to identify the ore.

On 23 April, the sun disappeared for the winter and the long polar night descended. Outside, the sea froze, and deep cold raged as if on an outer planet. For Shackleton and his men, the hut became their one citadel against the powers of Nature, the centre of their universe. There, the fifteen maroons, cooped up in too little space, had to cope with the strains of men constantly living cheek by jowl. It would have tried the patience of boon companions, but this company had been chosen on no obvious principle, except an obscure instinct, perhaps, for survivors.

There were evident divisions – like for example that between the Australians and the rest – and a web of subtler ones, shot with an unbalanced mind or two. Shackleton coped with them all. It was in this charged atmosphere, riddled with incompatibilities that he came into his own. There flared up within him the sacred flame of leadership. It was recognised by his companions. Whatever their private thoughts, at a deeper level, they were overcome by this singular force radiating from one man and dependent on no hierarchy. It kept them happy, or at least content, and subdued at least one outburst of violence. Those who had been on the previous expedition made comparisons with Scott, to Shackleton's unqualified advantage. He was by far the better leader of the two. For his part, Shackleton revealed his particular animus by laughing at Scott in private conversations. One of these was with Sir Philip Brocklehurst, educated at Eton and Trinity Hall, Cambridge, in whose person lay another sort of pioneer. He had made history by paying for a place on the expedition.

Shackleton had the true leader's vital gift of masking his worries, of which he had more than enough. Since landing, four horses had died, probably from eating volcanic grit. That left a slender margin of four for the polar journey. On that, Shackleton was staking fame and fortune. His chances were still further diminished by his company of novices. In the long morning twilight before the return of the sun on 22 August, Shackleton gave them their baptism of frost. It was too early and too cold, but he somehow meant to turn them into polar travellers in the few short months before the southern summer.

The training course was the few short miles over sea ice between Cape Royds and the old *Discovery*

quarters at the head of McMurdo Sound, where the Barrier debouched. There, Shackleton led the first party on 12 August. It was for him a bitter revival of old memories. He revisited the hut built there by Scott, but was quick to return to Cape Royds. Thereafter, every week, he sent out a party, but himself did not repeat the visit until 22 September, when he started on the single depot journey to bring supplies out to around 79°30' South latitude.

To begin with, he was accompanied by the stutter of a petrol engine. Shackleton had brought a motor car, yet another piece of pioneering. This was the first mechanical transport in Antarctica, although not in snow elsewhere. It was a piece of hasty improvisation. The vehicle was an ordinary open tourer, somewhat modified with runners on the front wheels to steer, and the engine altered to run in low temperatures. Shackleton imagined he would be able to drive effortlessly most of the way to the Pole. The first field trial, in February, soon after landing, disabused him of that notion. The car worked well enough on hard crust, but at the first sign of loose snow, the wheels spun helplessly, and it slithered to a halt. This happened again on the depot journey. The car actually carried the men and pulled their sledge for eight miles. Then they had to dismount and do their own hauling.

Ironically, despite his antagonism, Shackleton repeated many of Scott's mistakes. He used the same tight windclothes without hood attached and no fur, which guaranteed frostbite around the face. He persevered with the same clumsy tents. Again the winter had been frittered away in irrelevant activity. All too soon the spring arrived and the first party, ridiculously unprepared, set out. On 5 October, Edgeworth David, Douglas Mawson and the erratic junior doctor, Alistair Forbes Mackay, started off northwards to the South Magnetic Pole, which no one had yet reached. This was insurance, in case Shackleton did not reach the

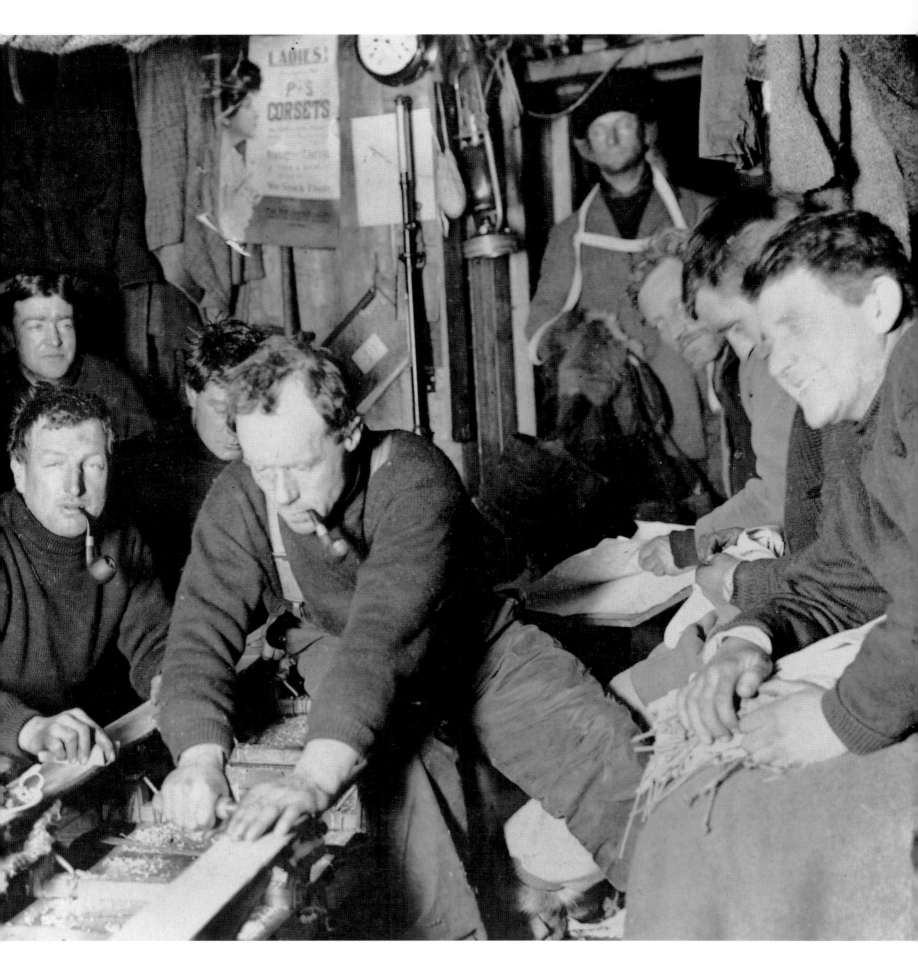

geographic Pole itself. David was the leader and he too started out with the motor car. All too soon he and his party had to hitch themselves to the sledge and prepare to man-haul every inch of the long trail ahead.

There was a repeat performance a few weeks later when, on 29 October, Shackleton finally started off for the South Pole, 747 nautical miles away. He and his companions led the four surviving horses. A support party of five were following in the car. With Ernest Joyce in command, it numbered Brocklehurst and Armitage, together with Raymond Priestley and George Marston, the expedition artist. Except for Joyce, they were polar tyros to a man. As usual, the car floundered at the first sign of drift, and was forced to turn, the driver, Bernard Day, bidding an ironic farewell. The passengers dismounted, hitched themselves to the sledge so hopefully hauled astern, and themselves began dragging by main force. At Cape Royds meanwhile, the dogs had been left, idle, whining, uneasy or at ease according to temperament.

The horses, poor devils, quickly showed their deficiencies in this alien world. They sank up to their hocks, or sometimes to their bellies, in the loose snow. The pressure on a horse's hoof was designed for other circumstances. What is more, a horse sweats through all his hide, so that once they stopped, the poor beasts froze. They had to be rubbed down and cosseted, whereas dogs would have looked after themselves. It was all a drain on the energies of the men, themselves floundering on foot, up to their ankles in snow, because of Shackleton's perverse prejudice against skis. The support party, struggling with a heavy sledge, were even worse off. They had become a hindrance. On 7 November, some fifty-five nautical miles out, Shackleton sent them back. He could only hope devoutly for their safe return to base.

Day after monotonous day, Shackleton now plodded on through the endless arid white wastes of the cold Antarctic desert, whipped by sharp-needled drift from the south like a sandstorm in the Sahara. On 25 November, he passed Scott's Furthest South of 82°17'. He had done so in only twenty-nine days, half the time Scott (and he) had taken in 1903. Henceforth, all was *terra incognita*.

Shackleton now knew the complex emotions of revenge. They masked danger signs. The horses were suffering from cold and exposure, and one of them, Chinaman, had already had to be put down. A few days after breaking the record, two more, Grisi and Quan, shared his fate, their carcasses also being

depoted as food for the return. So, early in the march, only one, known as Socks, was left. Shackleton had covered 380 miles, but there was still a good 360 more to go.

Men rather than animals were, however, the real concern. Under him, Shackleton had a heterogeneous trio. They were all misfits, one way or another. Socks belonged to Frank Wild, a Yorkshireman, a drifter on land, with a weakness for drink, who steadied and displayed a solid character only when civilisation had been left behind. Nominally second in command was a cantankerous, erratic former naval officer, John Boyd Adams. Finally came the senior expedition doctor, Eric Marshall, from Emmanuel College, Cambridge and Guys Hospital, London – a man with an unresolved streak of bitterness. Each to begin with had his own doubts about Shackleton; Marshall in particular suspected Shackleton of concealing ill-health. Shackleton tried to evade medical examination, but eventually Marshall managed to overcome his monumental reluctance. He discovered something indefinably wrong with his heart.

Gradually, however, Shackleton's extraordinary force of leadership won through. As new unnamed peaks drifted by on their right hand, the sensations of discovery overcame all. Still they did not know

whether the Pole lay on the rolling plain ahead or somewhere in the heights. On 3 December, came an answer of sorts. They climbed a low peak, dubbed Mount Hope, and this is what they saw. Sweeping away to the southeast were the summits of what are now called the Transantarctic Mountains. At their feet, a monstrous glacier ran upwards through the endless range.

Six years before, Shackleton had first seen the start of the road to the South. In the vast estuary of ice below him, he now found

Camp on the glacier below the mountain they christened 'The Cloudmaker'. Shackleton was using the same tent design as had been used on the Discovery *expedition, a cumbersome structure of five bamboo poles with the canvas shell thrown over and no fitted ground sheet. This meant that the snow and wind penetrated all too easily.*

its continuation. Again he was a precursor. There lay the highway running southwards. Here, perhaps was the key to the Pole. Where the temptation was to continue on the plain, he decided to strike up the glacier. It was an act of great courage, linked to intuition. It was also the beginning of his followers' submission to his leadership.

Under Mount Hope was the only observed pass on to the glacier, now called the Gateway. The glacier itself, Shackleton named Beardmore, after his patron. Along this glacier, Shackleton now led his men. On 7 December Socks, the last pony, broke through a snow bridge and disappeared into a crevasse. Luckily the trace broke, and the sledge was saved. It was hitched to the sledge hauled by Shackleton, Marshall and Adams since the other ponies had collapsed and, with Wild now hauling too, they continued dragging half a ton up to the heights. Without skis or crampons they floundered in snow or slithered on the ice where the wind had picked it clean.

The only sign of the accumulated lore of real snow travel was the sledges themselves. They were of a type with broad, ski-like runners, designed by Nansen twenty years before, and now standard for polar explorers, but their antecedents went back centuries among northern tribes. Shackleton had actually followed Scott on the obligatory brief pilgrimage to Nansen in Norway while preparing his own expedition – and then, like Scott, ignored most of his advice, especially on the use of skis and dogs.

Day after day, this strange quartet struggled ever upwards into the unknown, their own beasts of burden, wearing themselves out. They were at the limits of survival, and perhaps beyond. Their clothes let through the bitter wind, which burned through them with twenty and thirty degrees of frost. To eke out their supplies, Shackleton had cut down rations. Originally calculated for ninety-one days, he made them stretch for 125 to increase their chances of success. It was at the cost of literally starving. In the thin air, short of fuel to melt enough snow, they were suffering the subtle agonies of dehydration and also, as Marshall noted with disbelief, chronic hypothermia. He was most concerned by Shackleton, who was distressed by the altitude, and beginning to show every symptom of imminent collapse. Still Shackleton drove himself onwards.

On Christmas Day, having abandoned one sledge, he still believed that he could reach the Pole. On

Adams, Wild and Shackleton with Queen Alexandra's flag at Furthest South, 88°23'. Marshall took the photograph, on 9 January 1909. It was a bitter decision to have to turn back but Shackleton and his companions realised that to press on would have meant certain death.

the third day of the New Year, that delusion shattered. Marshall, the navigator, took a sun sight, giving a latitude of 87°22' South. The Pole was still 158 nautical miles off. Simple arithmetic told the tale. They could not now go the whole way and get back alive. The gradient admittedly had slackened, the surface smoothed out. They had emerged at last from the frozen cataracts of the Beardmore glacier, onto its very source, the Antarctic ice cap. They were at an altitude of more than 11,000 feet, and climbing still.

The only question now, as in 1902, was when to turn. Marshall wanted to do so then and there. Shackleton, having established a psychological mastery over the others, somehow drummed up their acquiescence, against their better judgement, to go on some way yet. As a consolation prize, he wanted to cross the magic line of the eighty-eighth parallel, and get within a hundred nautical miles of the Pole. On 7 January, his luck ran out. The good weather he had so far enjoyed broke, and a southerly storm kept them tent-bound for sixty hours.

Still Shackleton would not give up. When the wind dropped, he led his men – no, he carried them with his sheer willpower on a last southern dash. Leaving camp and sledge behind, and with nothing but a few biscuits for food, they hurried over the hard crust forged by the wind. After five hours they stopped. It was 9 January 1909. The latitude was 88°23' South.

That at least was what Marshall's dead reckoning said, and what Shackleton chose to believe. He had outdone Scott by six whole degrees of latitude, and got within ninety-seven miles of the Pole. He had more or less proved that it lay up on the ice cap discovered, incidentally, by Albert Armitage, his old friend on *Discovery*, six years before.

But all this was not victory, as Shackleton well knew. He had come as far as sheer courage could take him. His fate, after all, had been to show the way for others who might come after. Having quickly taken pictures, with Queen Alexandra's flag streaming in the breeze, he turned back almost within sight of the goal of his desires. It was surely one of the bravest acts in the history of polar exploration. To turn requires a special kind of courage – even if reinforced by outside persuasion.

From striving for success, Shackleton now plunged into the very different mental world of leading the flight back from extinction in the snows. It was a nightmare journey. Too tired to build cairns on the way

up, they had to depend for navigation on their tracks in the snow. On reaching the head of the Beardmore, they raced down pell-mell, regardless of snow bridges, ice falls, crevasses and the other assorted devilment of glaciers. Emaciated, frostbitten and starving, they looked like figures from a mythological scene that depicted a cold hell. Then on 20 January, halfway down, Shackleton collapsed.

Marshall, reflecting the natural hierarchy of the group, supplanted Adams, the nominal deputy and took command. For more than a week, Shackleton was desperately ill, struggling to breathe, well-nigh helpless, but somehow staggered on. To Marshall, it was the moment of disillusion. At one level, Shackleton had shown the triumph of the will; at another, he stood accused of irresponsibility. He was not physically fit for the tasks to which he had been driven by ambition, and knew it. In retrospect Marshall diagnosed a heart attack. If so, it was combined with lung trouble, altitude sickness and acute effort beyond his physical capacity. In any case, on 28 January, when at last they were down on the Barrier again, Shackleton recovered and resumed command.

The flight from extinction went on. It was a long forced march bedevilled by failing supplies and uncertainty. The season was on the wane. The difficulty of finding depots, poorly marked by single pennants like buoys in a storm, was an everlasting source of insecurity. As they hauled with fading strength on the sledge, they were being worn down. It was now, fighting against the odds, that Shackleton came into his own. He had trusted to luck to get him through, and uncannily the fickle weather held. Something within him now willed them all to survive.

Meanwhile he was hiding worries that were eating away at him from within. For one thing, he had told Ernest Joyce to lay a depot at a landmark called Minna Bluff. Shackleton absolutely depended on those supplies to avoid starvation and get through. The gnawing of that uncertainty only ceased on 23 February. On that day they found the depot, duly brought out by Joyce, by the aid incidentally of the dogs, last seen in repose at Cape Royds nearly four months before.

But Shackleton, however, now had another concern. He had left orders that if they had not returned by 1 March, they were to be written off and the relief ship could sail without them. They had eighty-five miles to go and barely a week in hand. Their desperate flight now transformed itself into a more orderly

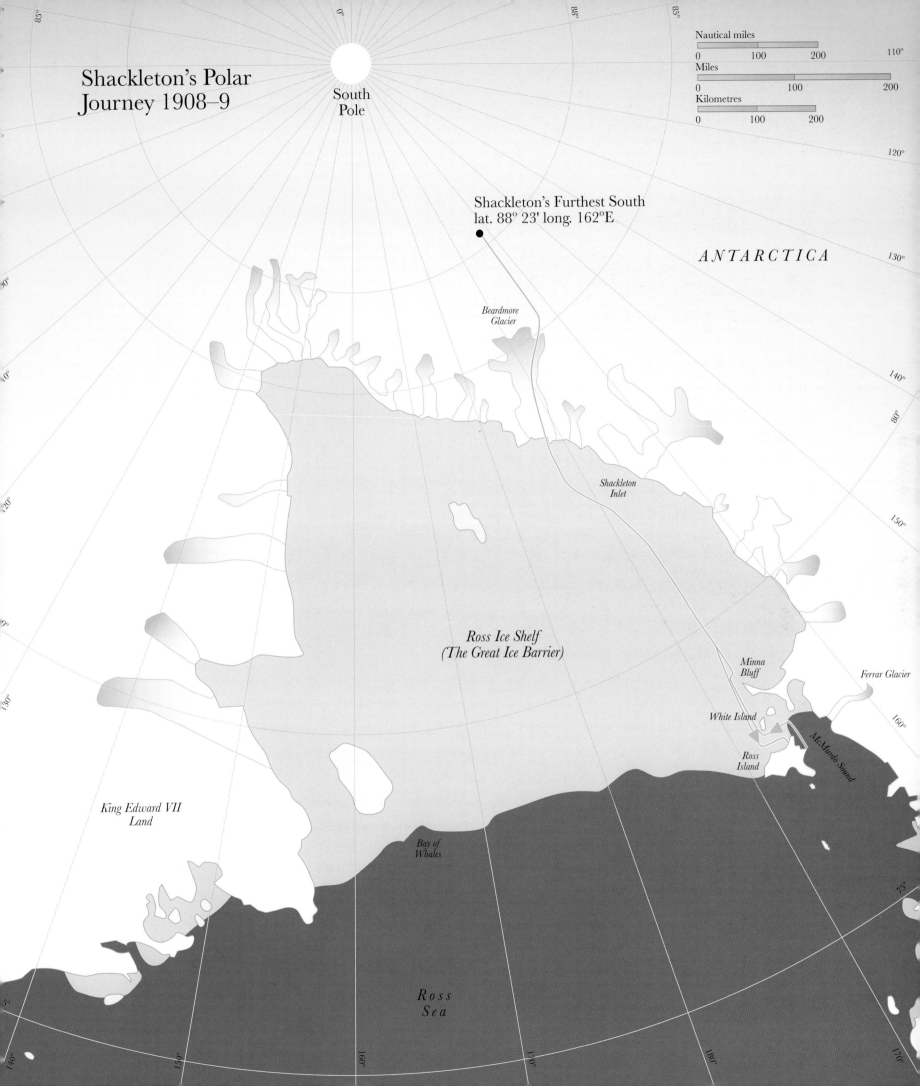

Shackleton's Polar
Journey 1908–9

South
Pole

Nautical miles
0   100   200

Miles
0   100   200

Kilometres
0   100   200

Shackleton's Furthest South
lat. 88° 23' long. 162°E

ANTARCTICA

Beardmore
Glacier

Shackleton
Inlet

Ross Ice Shelf
(The Great Ice Barrier)

Minna
Bluff

Ferrar Glacier

White Island

McMurdo Sound

Ross
Island

King Edward VII
Land

Bay of
Whales

Ross
Sea

race but, on their speed so far, it still promised a close call. They pressed on as fast as they could shuffle through the mocking snow, where skis would have carried them at ease. And then it was Marshall's turn to be ill, unexpectedly overcome by violent cramps and dysentery. This slowed them down and, on 27 February he collapsed, bringing them all to a halt, still over thirty miles from safety.

Leaving Marshall behind with Adams to nurse him, Shackleton and Wild rushed on ahead to try to catch the ship. Still his luck with the weather held. The snow remained as crust and there was a following wind. Half running, half stumbling for thirty-six hours with a few hours' rest, the pair staggered on to Hut Point, where lay the old *Discovery* hut. Frozen and starving – Adams had egregiously packed only enough food for a day – they were at the end of their tether. It was midnight on the last day of February, just within the time agreed, but no ship was there.

Outwardly undaunted, Shackleton kept up the appearance of hope and, next morning, *Nimrod* duly appeared out of the mist. Shackleton went on board, like the leader returning from the dead. He found something like near mutiny. When *Nimrod* sailed back to New Zealand, she carried sealed orders from

Shackleton to dismiss Rupert England, her original Captain, whom Shackleton had accused of being too timid in landing the party. The new Captain was Frederick Pryce Evans, who had commanded the *Koonya*, the vessel that had towed *Nimrod* on the way out. But he now showed similar failings, in addition to overriding Shackleton's orders for his relief. This included sending out a search party if he had not returned by 25 February, besides keeping Hut Point provisioned and manned. It was deserted when Shackleton arrived. It was thanks to the insistence of men fiercely loyal to Shackleton that *Nimrod* now appeared at all.

Shackleton's chagrin at not having succeeded in his quest was partially mitigated by Edgeworth David's doing so in his. David had indeed reached the South Magnetic Pole. He had done what he intended, and thus fulfilled the definition of success. That was true of something else as well. Before the onset of winter, a party under Adams and David had made the first ascent of Mount Erebus, thereby achieving also the first ascent of an Antarctic peak into the bargain. Nor was Shackleton there either. Of his power of leadership now there could be no doubt, but his actual presence on the ground seemed somehow to be a curse.

By now Shackleton had had hardly any rest for the best part of two and a half days. Nonetheless he kept going. He seemed to have recovered from whatever it was that had nearly destroyed him barely a month before. Even Wild had become exhausted to the point of collapse. He remained on board when Shackleton, accompanied by Mawson and Mackay, immediately went out to rescue Marshall and Adams. On 3 March, rescuers and rescued finally returned to Hut Point, Marshall by then having improved sufficiently to move under his own steam. *Nimrod*, having sheered off, picked them up after an interval.

The Antarctic by then seemed to have spent its spleen. *Nimrod* had an easy passage back to civilisation. At last on 23 March, she arrived at Halfmoon Bay on Stewart Island, and Shackleton duly went ashore to send his cable.

'I am missing you more than ever and the only thing that keeps me from worrying over going is that I have to carry on working: it has made such an awful blank in my life and I feel that I never realised all you were to me and all the children were though I was so fond of you. I can really and truly promise darling that when I come back again I will never go away from you.'

From Shackleton's letter to Emily Shackleton, written on a liner going to Australia, 5 November 1907

'. . . the small snapshot of you I am going to take with me on the journey so that your picture will be one that will reach the Pole if the Gods are kind.'

Shackleton's letter to Elspeth Beardmore (Lady Invernairn), 5 November 1907

1 Shackleton's decision to take horses rather than dogs to the Antarctic is not easy to understand. On Shackleton's visit to Nansen in Norway the latter had introduced him to an experienced dog handler, who failed to persuade Shackleton of the breed's virtues. Instead Shackleton ordered Manchurian ponies, which were shipped to New Zealand from Tientsin in China and trained to run with sledges out on Quail Island.

2 At the last minute, perhaps with Nansen's urgings still echoing in his ears, Shackleton decided to take nine sledge dogs with him on *Nimrod*. The only person on the expedition with any experience of these animals was Joyce, who had been on *Discovery*, and that had not been a particularly auspicious start to dog driving.

1

2

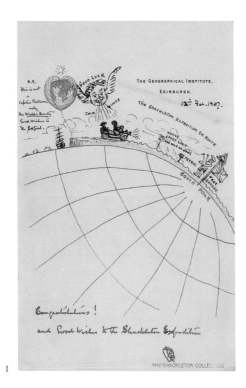

I

3

1 'Congratulations! And good wishes to the Shackleton Expedition.' This note came from an unidentified correspondent at the Geographical Institute in Edinburgh and shows the expedition driving to the South Pole (with a waiting Scotsman) in Shackleton's motor car. The inclusion of the car had caused great interest prior to the expedition sailing and was the subject of a feature in the *Illustrated London News*.

2 Cargo boxes being loaded at Lyttelton Harbour or a lesson into how to cram a quart into a pint pot. *Nimrod* was 'impressively overloaded'. In addition to all the food and equipment for the human members of the expedition, she was carrying the motor car in its crate and the ponies with their bales of hay.

3 *Nimrod* left Lyttelton Harbour amidst a fanfare of optimism on New Year's Day 1908. Some 30,000 people had turned up to see Ernest Shackleton and his expedition set sail for the Antarctic. There was a real sense of expectation that this might lead to the South Pole and glory.

1 Unlike the party aboard *Discovery*, which was largely made up of naval officers, the officers of *Nimrod* came from a great variety of backgrounds. On their way down to New Zealand, when most of them met for the first time, they discovered each other's flaws and strengths, so that by the time Shackleton joined the ship in Lyttelton the rivalries and friendships were already well established.

2 Sir Philip Brocklehurst was just nineteen when he first met Shackleton. The son of a wealthy Staffordshire family, he was inspired by Shackleton's bohemian character, as he described it, to join him on *Nimrod*. His mother contributed funds towards Shackleton's venture and thus Brocklehurst became the first in a long tradition of explorers who helped to underwrite the cost of the expeditions they joined.

3 The sextant is an optical instrument which (combined with a chronometer for establishing accurate time) determines position by measuring the angular attitude of heavenly bodies. It is adapted for use on board ship since the user can level it manually to compensate for any movement. The advantage of the sextant is that it is quick and relatively easy to use. A sextant was carried by the astronauts of the Apollo 11 mission to the moon to cross-check the computer's navigational readings.

2

3

1 A man climbing the rigging.

2 Priestley, a young student from University College Bristol, was selected as the expedition's geologist. He learned of his acceptance when he received a telegram from Shackleton asking why he had not yet collected his equipment from London. An astute observer of human nature, he made some perceptive and often witty remarks about his companions.

3 The sky, full of skuas and petrels, was one of the great beauties of the southern seas. These birds spend almost the whole of their lives on the wing, flying distances that are almost incalculable.

3

2

1 Voyagers' diaries often noted the millpond-like conditions of the Ross Sea in front of the Barrier. However, the sea around King Edward VII Land was more treacherous, particularly so when the pack ice threatened to crush *Nimrod* against the Barrier.

2 When Shackleton returned to the Barrier in 1908 he was surprised to see that a huge section of it had calved, revealing a new bay. The calving also produced a significant number of large icebergs, which, as ever, presented a threat to the ship.

1 The ship's path through the pack ice left a
 black trail that stretched into the distance.
 The slosh and occasional groan of the ice
 colliding with the ship was a sound new to
 many of the party. As they sailed on the ice
 closed slowly behind them, cutting them off
 from the outside world.

2 At least once *Nimrod* was threatened with
 being crushed by the pack ice. Her Captain,
 Rupert England, realised that the ship could
 not move under sail alone, and he was
 anxious about the amount of coal he had
 left for the return journey to New Zealand.

3 The nervous England had no intention of
 allowing himself or his ship to be trapped in
 the ice for the winter, and so several
 attempts were made to find a suitable place
 for the landing party to get ashore.

4 Shackleton took out a small boat to sound
 the approaches to Cape Royds to see if
 they could put ashore there. The need to
 find somewhere safe to unload the winter
 supplies was taxing Shackleton and
 vexing England.

3

4

Previous page: Shackleton had been forced to promise Scott that he would not land at McMurdo Sound but *Nimrod* had become jammed against the pack ice in an attempt to reach King Edward VII Land. With a heavy heart Shackleton realised he had no option but to go back on his word and overwinter on the eastern side of Ross Island after all.

1 Fish caught at Cape Royds with a fish trap. Raymond Priestley's notes to the photograph read: 'They were bottom fish living at a depth of thirty-four fathoms (or 204 feet). The fish-trap was made of copper wire and was circular, with two small entrances, exit being prevented by conveying spikes inwards.'

2 As expedition geologist Priestley found that he had ample excuse to take himself away from the rest of his companions in search of scientific material. He always carried his camera with him, and some of the most atmospheric and evocative photographs from the voyage come from his forays inland or along the shore.

2

1 On one of his expeditions from the hut,
  Raymond Priestley came upon this glacier
  melt-water lake.
2 Priestley captioned this extraordinary
  photograph, 'Frozen ponies breath on the
  roof of the stables . . . FACT! I assure you'.
  The ponies were kept in a stable next to
  the car garage, where they were fed on
  hay. Gradually they became ill, and it was
  Priestley who discovered that they were
  eating volcanic grit. By mid-March three
  of them had died, leaving only five for
  the Southern Journey.
3 This photograph of James Murray and
  Priestley in a trench in Green Lake was
  taken in June 1908 by the light of hurricane
  lamps. Priestley recorded that 'the
  temperature was –22°F and we sat for ten
  minutes; such agonies will ordinary mortals
  undergo for the pleasure of having their
  faces perpetuated.'

3

1

1, 2 Among the collection of photographs taken by Priestley were striking images of snow crystals and ice formations in caves. In suitable conditions, such as in the shelter of a cave, the crystals grew to a large size in multifarious but defined patterns. Against the glow of the hurricane lamp, they look almost other-worldly.

3 The end of the glacier showing the large amount of moraine that accumulates. In the foreground are snow flowers. This photograph appears in *The Heart of the Antarctic* Vol. 1 and is captioned 'ice flowers on newly formed sea ice in the early winter'.

2

4

1 During the Antarctic winter the hours of daylight were short and very precious, but with the Aurora Australis (southern lights) they produced some of the loveliest scenes. Here it is early spring and the sun is returning.

2 Frank Wild dressed in winter rig. He had been a close companion to Shackleton on the *Discovery* expedition and had jumped at the chance of joining *Nimrod* when invited. He became Shackleton's most loyal right-hand man and was distinguished by being the only one of Shackleton's men to join all four of his expeditions.

3 Penguin meat made a welcome change from seal and was added to the men's diet soon after landing at Cape Royds. Shackleton had been convinced on *Discovery* that fresh meat had been the secret of keeping scurvy at bay. On *Nimrod* he had an ally in Marshall, who had done research on the subject. So sure was Shackleton of the link between fresh fruit and meat and the disease that he organised for tinned fruit and tomatoes to be included in their supplies.

4 Mount Erebus was a constant presence, along with the penguins who congregated around it. The rumbles from the bowels of the volcano, coupled with the sporadic clouds of steam pouring forth from it, gave some indication of the very great power that lay below.

1 An assortment of ramshackle buildings housed the car, in the small garage to the left, and the Manchurian ponies, who had stalls in the hut block next door.

2 The Emperor penguins were particularly inquisitive and unafraid. The dogs attracted their attention and vice versa, but the penguins tended to win the battle of nerves.

3 A subject of great interest for the public in Britain and for the penguins in the Antarctic, the motor car performed very well on the firm ice but on soft snow it was rendered useless.

2

3

1 Priestley and the three sledge dogs, Cis, Erebrus and Possum, photographed next to a snow cliff and cornice. According to Priestley, the cornice 'was one of the best we met with'. The honeycombed appearance of the cliff, he noted, was due to the combined effect of sun and wind.

2, 3 The so-called Igloo Hut was used to store provisions for the expedition. Whenever a blizzard blew the soft, dry snow entered all the nooks and crannies, leaving everything inside covered in a fine coating of white powder.

4 Inside the hut at Cape Royds a watchman sits in front of the stove while Marston reads. The tall boiler contains water for the ponies, while the smaller one holds water for the men.

5 'The Old Curiosity Shop.' Edgeworth David, a dignified man and a peacemaker, shared this tiny cramped cubicle with Douglas Mawson, his fellow Australian. Together they made the ascent of Mount Erebus and the discovery of the South Magnetic Pole.

3

4

5

1 Joyce and Wild in 'Rogue's Retreat', as Priestley described it, working on harnesses with a treadle sewing machine. The cubicle measured six feet six inches wide. In these cramped conditions, in which the two men lived together for seven months or more, they set themselves up as printers, having undertaken a crash course in printing before leaving England.

2 Lithographs, such as this printing device of two penguins, were produced in the Hut.
3 This programme marks the occasion of one of the 'wild sprees' that punctuated an otherwise teetotal régime. It was a tradition among the Antarctic expeditions to celebrate Midwinter's Day in June, and the festivities often included a production of sorts as well as dinner.

BRITISH ANTARCTIC EXPEDITION. 1907.

MIDWINTER CELEBRATION.
AT WINTER QUARTERS,
CAPE ROYDS.
LAT. 77°·· 32′ S.
LONG. 166°·· 12′ E.
JUNE 23RD. 1908.

"When the shadow of night's eternal wings
    Envelopes the gloomy whole,
And the mutter of deep-mouth'd thunderings
    Shakes all the starless pole."
                — TENNYSON.

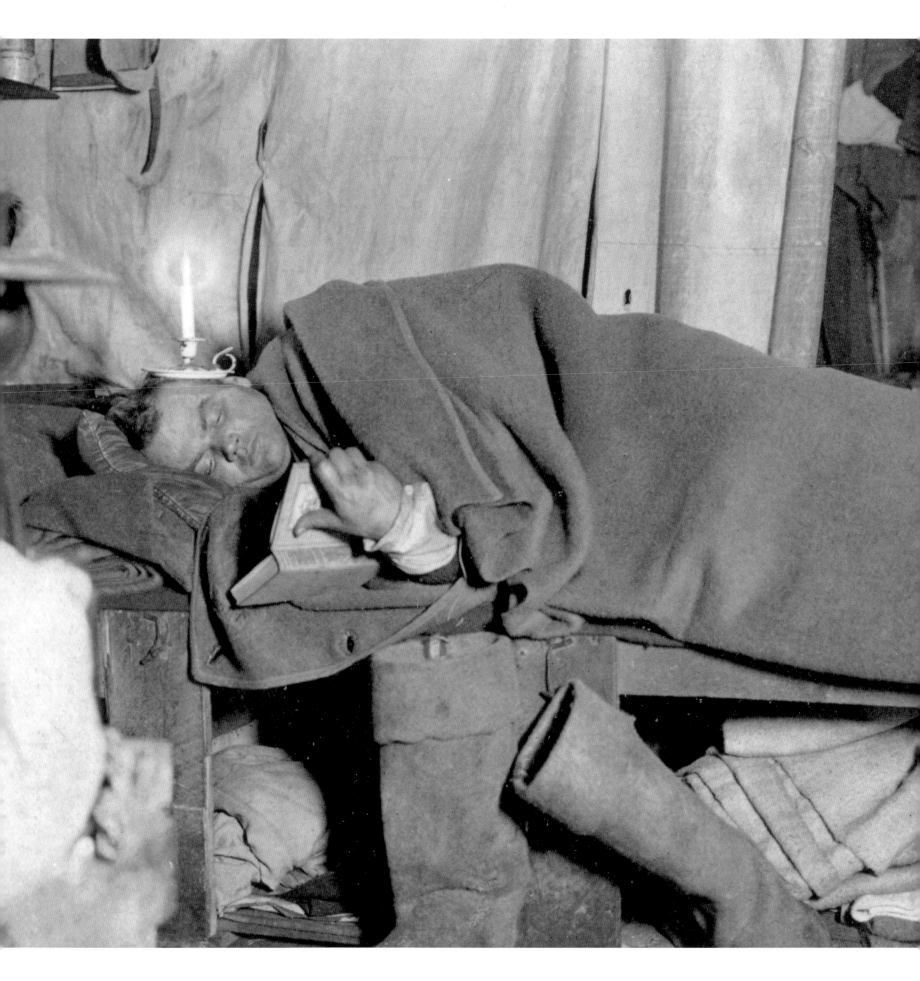

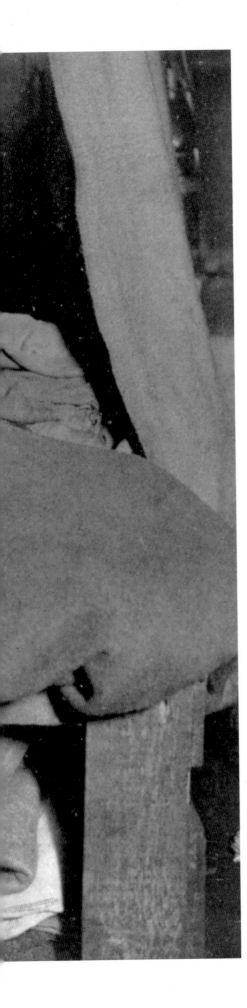

1 George 'Putty' Marston was the expedition's artist. Raymond Priestley wrote that Marston had the 'frame and face of a prizefighter and the disposition of a fallen angel'.

2 Alistair Forbes Mackay taking a bath, June 1908. Washing was a luxury, for every drop of water had to be collected as ice and melted.

2

1 Mount Erebus erupted spectacularly from 8.20 to 8.40 pm on 14 June 1908, giving a show equal to that of the Aurora Australis.

2 The Aurora Australis gleamed and flickered like an ethereal curtain in the Antarctic sky. Sometimes the display would last for hours on end; then it would fade, only to return unexpectedly and more strongly. The aurora (Borealis or Australis) is caused by charged particles from the sun colliding with gas molecules in the atmosphere. Bursts of these particles are associated with displays which is why they are not constant.

1 Shackleton and comrades with the four
remaining Manchurian ponies just before
setting off on the Southern Journey.
2 This picture is the first of a series of
photographs (pages 138–46) taken from
an album that Shackleton himself

prepared and captioned to present to his
friend Lord Dudley in 1909. This
photograph was taken at the start of the
journey. Next to it Shackleton wrote: 'Final
start of Southern Party. The Queen's flag
ahead, our sledge flags flying.'

'As we left the Hut where we spent so many months in comfort we all felt a real feeling of regret for never again would we all be together there. It was dark inside and the acetylene [lamp] was feeble in comparison to the sun outside and it was small compared to any wooden dwelling yet we were sad at leaving . . . At 10 [am] we . . . said goodbye then went on our way . . . those who were left had done for me all that man could do in their own particular work to try and make our little expedition a success. The clasp of the hand means more than many words.'

From Shackleton's sledging diary, at the start of the Southern Journey, 29 October 1908

'It is 750 miles as the crow flies from our winter quarters to the Pole and we have only done 51 of them as yet. But still the worst will turn to the best I doubt not. That a Polar Explorer needs a large stock of patience in his equipment there is no denying . . . I read some of Shakespeare's Comedies today.'

From Shackleton's diary, 8 November 1908

1 The Southern Party at camp at 82°45′ South, having broken the previous Furthest South record. A few days earlier, on 20 November 1908, Shackleton had written in his diary: 'It seems as though we were truly at the world's end and were bursting in on the birthplace of the clouds and the nesting home of the four winds and that we mortals were being watched with a jealous eye by these children of Nature.'

2 The tents, at the camp on the Lower Glacier, were pitched on the moraine with a backdrop of granite rock that stood over 1,200 feet high.

'The outstanding feature of today's march is that we have seen new land to the South never seen by human eyes before great snow clad heights [which] we did not see on our journey South on the last Expedition for we were too close to the land or rather foothills and now at the great distance we are out they can be plainly seen.'

From Shackleton's diary, 22 November 1908

1, 2 The land Shackleton and his men were now seeing was completely new and uncharted. As Shackleton admitted in his diary, its vastness and the extraordinary beauty of the isolation briefly took their minds off their hunger: 'We are ever adding to the chain of wonderful mountains we have found. At one moment our thoughts are in the grandeur of the scene the next of what we would like to eat . . . for we are very hungry and we know that we are likely to be for another three months.'

1 Mount Hope was the name given
spontaneously to the 2,000-foot rock island
Shackleton's party scrambled up only to
see the enormous glacier that would give
them access through the Transantarctic
Mountains. Although they had hoped to
find a mountain pass, the glacier was,
nevertheless, one of the only gaps
Shackleton and his men were technically
capable of negotiating.

2 This spectacular granite cliff provided the
team with a useful landmark, as well as a
site on the glacier to place a camp. Here
they laid their fourth depot of the journey
and, with a lightened load, continued up
the glacier.

1

'The worst feature of today's
march was the terribly soft snow in
the hollows of the great undulations
we were crossing during the
afternoon. One was so bad that the
ponies sank in right up to their bellies.
[They] were played out by 5.45 [pm]
especially old Quan who nearly
collapsed not from the weight of the
sledge but lifting his feet and limbs
through the soft snow.'

From Shackleton's diary, 29 November 1908

'Hard is the fight and we can but do our best we can go on and on till the food is nearly spent then we must turn. Please God we will win through.'

From Shackleton's diary, 12 December 1908

1 This photograph was taken by Shackleton on Christmas Day 1908, 10,000 feet up on the Great Glacier, now known as the Beardmore Glacier after the Scottish industrialist who helped fund the *Nimrod* expedition.

2 Shackleton named a section of the Transantarctic Mountains the 'Queen Alexandra Mountains', for it was she who had given him her flag which he would raise at his Furthest South. He carried the flag with him and was photographed with it at 88°23' South.

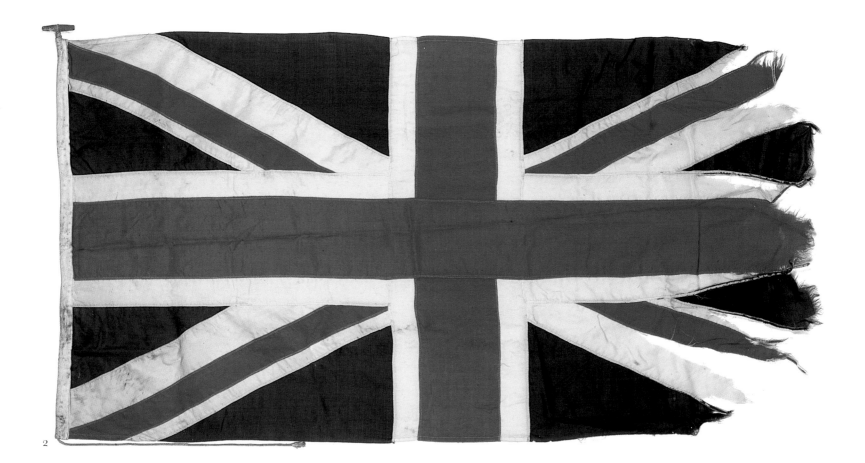

3 On 30 December 1908 a great blizzard blew up and for the first time for more than six weeks the men were held weatherbound in their tents. Shackleton's patience was tested and he wrote in his diary that night: 'All day we have been lying in our sleeping bags trying to keep warm and listening to the threshing drift on the tent side . . . Our precious food is going and our time also . . . It lies with Providence to help us more.'

'The last day out . . . The wind eased down at 1 am and at 2 am we were up had breakfast and shortly after 4 am started south with the Union Jack and the brass cylinder of stamps. At 9 am quick hard marching we were in 88°23' and there hoisted HM's flag took possession of the Plateau in the name of HM and called it KE. Plat. Rushed back over a surface hardened somewhat by recent wind and had lunch took photo of camp Furthest South: and then got away marching til 5 pm dead tired camped lovely night . . . Homeward bound. Whatever regrets may be we have done our best.'

From Shackleton's diary, 9 January 1909

1 The 'Furthest South' sledge, which according to Shackelton's diary was 'in a v. shaky state', just about survived the descent of the Beardmore Glacier. It would not run straight and was a severe trial to the hungry men.

2 The weak and starving men reached the depot at Minna Bluff on 22 February 1908 at 4.30 pm. There they found not only rations but little delicacies which seemed to them immeasurably sweet and delicious after months of perpetual hunger. The message left at the depot by Joyce informed them that *Nimrod* was due to sail on 1 March.

3 After three months on the march *Nimrod* felt wonderfully luxurious. Shackleton was aware, however, of the need to return quickly to civilisation to spread the word of their Southern Journey. He would be a hero, he knew, but briefly, for there would surely be another attempt on the Pole.

'Child I cannot say how I feel about all the worry to you but it is over now Sweeteyes and all will go well you can judge this from the cables re lectures book etc. The Expedition has been a success darling though we did not get the Pole I did my best I *had* to come back to you and our children.'

From Shackleton's letter to Emily Shackleton, written from New Zealand, 1 April 1909

4

SIR ERNEST SHACKLETON, THE CELEBRITY

Opposite: Shackleton dressed for his part as a celebrity following his Furthest South record of 87°22'.
Right: The souvenir album was given to Shackleton as a welcome by the Explorers Club of New York on 29 March 1910 and the menus include one from a celebratory dinner held in his honour at the Transportation Club, New York on 30 March 1910.

Shackleton arrived back in London on 14 June 1909 to a national orgy of triumphalism, masking intimations of self-doubt. There were fears of a decline in British military and industrial might and fears of German aggression. There were even the now familiar fears of global warming, based on the calving of the Ross Ice Barrier that produced the Bay of Whales. Shackleton's achievement was exactly the antidote to the mood of national neurosis. The German threat already loomed large. But in polar exploration at least, as the Press comfortingly boasted, Britain still reigned supreme.

The frenzy revolved round the person of Shackleton. He was the hero of the hour. He was more. He was a reassuring figure for an age of doubt. His sturdy build contradicted alarms over national physical decay. His energy, his singular personality, the mark of an iron will, suggested a throwback to other and more certain times. His theatricality and poetic tastes invited comparison with the first Elizabethans. Such was the publicly simple figure, with his hidden complexities, striding out to enjoy his season of fame.

Shackleton tore round from dinners to receptions and luncheons. Fashionable hostesses vied for his charismatic presence. Everybody wanted to share in his celebrity. By virtue of his birth, the Irish too adopted him as a local hero of their own; but Anglo-Irish as he was, Shackleton did not wholly reciprocate that favour. Elsewhere there was more to gain. Shackleton had plunged frenziedly into a race to profit from his attainment before he was inevitably eclipsed. He had the mysterious power of transmuting success into triumph. It was a gift not given to all, least of all to Scott, on whom Shackleton now had at least temporary revenge.

It was not only that Shackleton had broken the record for the Furthest South. For the moment, he was the man who had been closest to either pole of the Earth. What is more, by advancing 360 miles, he had made the biggest single stride towards both poles that had ever been, or, given the short distances that remained, ever could be made. That record, at least, he would never lose.

Triumph was, however, mysteriously flawed. Still there remained that little lap to the South Pole itself. Shackleton was haunted by the fact that he had struggled only to show someone else the way, and that that someone, would after all, it seemed, be Scott. Scott was now about to make his second attempt on the Pole. Shackleton, despite a promise to his wife that he would never again leave her for the snows, was already toying with the idea of another expedition. His plans proved abortive, but once again Scott extracted from him a written promise that he would not return to McMurdo Sound. Unconscious that he himself was playing with the Fates, Scott wanted a signature to seal that bargain too.

Scott announced his new expedition on 12 September 1909. A little earlier, the Americans Dr F.A. Cook and R.E. Peary had returned to civilisation, both claiming to have reached the North Pole. These were acute reminders to polar explorers that time was running out.

Shackleton made sure that at least some of his companions accompanied him on the social round to share in his season of glory. It was an expression of his very genuine care for the men under his command. That also had counted in his decision to turn at the Furthest South. On a different note he explained to his wife that he thought she would prefer a live donkey to a dead lion.

The British press begged to disagree. It was Shackleton's near disaster and suffering in the snows that really made his name. There was little public praise for his courage in turning back – the greatest courage of

Shackleton and his long-suffering wife taking a walk in the streets of Dover the day after his return from his expedition to the South Pole.

all. Nor was he given credit for bringing everyone back alive. In fact, his was the first Antarctic expedition to return without losing a man. Scott had lost two on *Discovery*. But Shackleton's talent for survival was somehow considered bad form. Comparisons were made with sacrificial icons such as Livingstone and Gordon of Khartoum. The public knew that there was no hero like a dead hero. Meanwhile, Scott and his supporters, headed by Sir Clements Markham, the most fanatical of them all, were slyly doing their best to discredit Shackleton.

First of all his honesty was impugned because he had broken his promise to avoid McMurdo Sound. Then he was rumoured to have faked his latitudes. The Royal Geographical Society, having first kept their distance and now wishing to share in his reflected glory, actually gave their authoritative approval up to Marshall's last sun sight at 87°22'. The question was reduced to what happened after that. Shackleton was hurt, but a national hero he still remained.

When Shackleton returned, he was like a privateer sailing back into port. He had, after all, financed his expedition by very private enterprise, and he was deeply in debt. In the middle of August, the Liberal Government, submitting to popular opinion, made him a grant of £20,000. This more or less covered the deficit. Meanwhile, a month previously, Shackleton found himself made a Companion of the Royal Victorian Order. This was obviously to put him on a par with Scott on his return on *Discovery*. However, in November Shackleton went one better. He was knighted in the Birthday Honours List. Now he was Sir Ernest Shackleton, while Scott was still plain Captain. King Edward VII, that astute and underrated monarch, evidently knew much more than he cared to reveal about what was happening beneath the surface.

But now there was the future to consider. Since returning to New Zealand, Shackleton had been writing, or rather dictating, the book of the expedition. As *The Heart of the Antarctic*, it was published in London during November. It had taken a mere five months to write and produce. It received both public and critical acclaim, but its publication also marked the end of the original great surge of welcome. It had coincided with a tragic aftermath of the expedition. Away in Australia, Bertram Armytage committed suicide, another victim, perhaps in polar mania, and a reminder of its cost in human terms.

Shackleton's companions left the social round to return to everyday life. To his own restless nature that was an alien concept. He had to continue profiting from his Furthest South while the going was good. Early in November, he began on that bane of the times, the repetitive, self-promoting lecture tour. Nobody knows what tedium the modern celebrity has been saved in personal appearances by the advent of television, able as it is to reach the world at the cost of a single more or less harrowing session. Shackleton was booked to appear more than a hundred times in six months, over two continents, and to travel thousands of miles not, of course, by air, but lengthily by sea and land.

Abroad, Shackleton was able to prolong the season of acclaim, without the bitter pinpricks inflicted on him at home. Foreigners simply wanted a heroic explorer of conspicuous achievement, and that is what they got. A blend of genial privateer and man of action, larger than life with the common touch, he had a triumphal progress. From the strident patriots of Berlin, to the tragic figure of the last Tzar, Nicholas II in St Petersburg, Shackleton charmed them all. By way of a lecture tour in America, he returned to London in the middle of June 1910.

It was a surprisingly different place from that which he had left a few short months before. King Edward VII had died, and with him the Edwardian era, of which Shackleton had been such an ornament. Now he was somehow out of time and out of place. War was imminent and, in the more serious reign of George V, Shackleton found himself more evidently baffled. His enemies, who were fanning the undercurrent of suspicion, felt by contrast reinforced.

The fact was that Shackleton had become involved in various shady money-making schemes backed, when not actually fronted, by his brother Frank. As these enterprises had failed Shackleton became embroiled in the disreputable consequences. Behind the public hero, Shackleton now appeared a little decayed. This aspect of his personality ashore was sadly at variance with his more likeable self afloat.

He was noticeably restless and chafing under domesticity. He had left Edinburgh and, after various moves, in June 1911, he set up house in Putney, in relatively smart southwest London. By his own admission, however, he did not see much of his family. He had never put down roots. Emily had to support herself and her children with her own income, helped by her brother.

Shackleton only knew that his triumph was necessarily waning. Scott was now in the Antarctic, trying for the Pole. So, unexpectedly, was the masterly Norwegian, Roald Amundsen. Scott's expedition had turned into a race. The end came with the news early in March 1912 that Amundsen had reached the Pole on 14 December 1911. He had won. A few weeks later, Scott's expedition ship *Terra Nova* reached the cablehead with proof that he had lost. That, for Shackleton, was the really important news. The mere thought of being forced to give way to Scott had been unbearable. Amundsen had saved him from that humiliation and been indeed the agent of Shackleton's ultimate revenge. Consequently, Shackleton was one of the few publicly to support Amundsen among the huffy national chorus of chagrin.

Still Shackleton bore the burden of the man who had struggled, only to show the way ahead. It was at least now lightened on two counts. To adapt a saying of Napoleon, one could be vanquished by a man like Amundsen without disgrace. Besides, Amundsen always paid his historical debts. He acknowledged what he owed to Shackleton. He did so generously in the book of his expedition, published in English as *The South Pole*. The other, wry consolation to Shackleton was that Amundsen had pioneered a completely new route from the Bay of Whales, whereas Scott had followed in his former rival's tracks almost every inch of the way. The landmarks were where Shackleton had indicated, and Scott had to swallow his words, confirming the truth of everything Shackleton had said.

In fact, after the first wave of disappointment, Scott was gradually dismissed as an also-ran. That too consoled Shackleton. But in February 1913, with the return to New Zealand for the second time of *Terra Nova*, bringing the news that Scott had reached the Pole weeks after Amundsen, but had perished with all his companions on the way back, the public mood changed again. Shackleton happened to be in America on one of his hopeful business trips at the time. On his return, he pointedly told a journalist that of the three men, Scott, Wilson and himself, who had been at the Furthest South in 1903, only he Shackleton

Shackleton met Robert Peary in Philadelphia in 1910 when he was making a lecture tour of the United States. Peary claimed to have reached the North Pole in 1909. The two men met again, in 1913, when they were briefly together with Amundsen, who was on his own US lecture tour, having reached the South Pole on 14 December 1911.

had now survived – Wilson having perished with Scott – and he was the one written off at the time as an invalid. This did him little good. He was puzzled as well as galled by the morbid public adulation of the dead hero, who by his own incompetence had brought disaster on himself and his own men. Shackleton also disapproved of the grudging reception accorded to Amundsen, who had won with insulting ease.

However he looked at it, Shackleton now suffered the bitter eclipse of the precursor. His Furthest South was now receding into history, his present troubles were mounting up. He was having an affair with the American-born Rosalind Chetwynd and the strain of keeping up appearances with Emily was telling. There remained the mysterious shadow over his health. His business affairs were in disarray. The geological samples which, at the risk of his life, he had brought back all the way from the environs of the Beardmore Glacier had revealed no trace of economically viable minerals, much less of gold or precious stones. Antarctica had not been his Eldorado after all. Worse still, his brother Frank had been sent to prison for fraud, although he himself had not been publicly implicated. He had become a hanger-on of rich men, and depended more or less on their benevolence for pocket money, as it were.

Shackleton, however, was not the man to allow past grievance or present difficulty to destroy his hunger for achievement. Four years of being a looker-on was more than he could bear. When the news of Amundsen's triumph arrived in March 1912, Shackleton could not deny that it had taken the gloss off polar exploration, but he publicly denied that it would mean the end. The next great exploit, he announced, would be the crossing of Antarctica from sea to sea, passing the South Pole on the way. That was what he now proposed to do. In this way only could he retrieve his rightful fame. He was in search of his lost youth. Like a whirlwind, once more, he swept into action.

'I really do not know anything of a first success, although I am quite well aware that the people who have been good enough to concern themselves with my work would consider that I ought to regard my Antarctic expedition in that light. And, indeed I feel that it has been successful, but it was not the work of a moment.

'Success in an expedition of that sort can only be gained by two great forces. The first of these is attention to detail and organisation, and the second to the co-operation of good men. The good men I certainly had with me, so that if the expedition is my first success, they share it with me.

'All success, however, has its limitations, and a man may do good work without of necessity considering that it is a "First" success. For my own part, I believe that when a man begins his life-work young, and has the definite carrying-out of an object in view for which he feels fitted, his success must come gradually, and be quite unlike that indefinite thing which is the result, say, of putting one's money on a race-horse or into a gold mine and saying that that speculation or investment was one's first success.'

Interview with Shackleton, periodical 'M.A.P.', after *Nimrod*, headlined 'In the Days of my Youth. My First Success', 2 July 1909

VOLCANIC MOUNTAIN M⁺ EREBUS ASCENDED
SOUTH MAGNETIC POLE DISCOVERED
WITHIN 90 MILES SOUTH POLE.

·N·

NIMROD.

LIEUT. E. SHACKLETON.
COMMANDER of EXPEDITION.

THE RETURN of THE BRITISH ANTARCTIC EXPEDITION.
LYTTLETON MARCH 1909.
N.Z.

Previous page: Honours awaited Shackleton on his return from the Furthest South. He was awarded the CVO in July 1909 and in November he was knighted in the King's Birthday Honours. The *Daily Mirror* reported with genuine enthusiasm, 'none of the honours will be more popular with the public'. Shackleton had become a national hero.

1 'The Return of the British Antarctic Expedition, Lyttelton, New Zealand, March 1909.' This sketch summed up the achievement of the expedition and began the publicity offensive that culminated in a rapturous homecoming to London in the late summer of 1909.

2 The hero returned from Antarctica to be met with scenes of jubilation at home. Crowds thronged the streets, pushing forward to get a glimpse of the man who had got closer to the South Pole than any other in history. He was the man of the moment and he relished it.

1 All summer Shackleton was feted and 'his diary read like the roll-call of society'. Emily was for once able to benefit from her husband's extraordinary career and she accompanied him whenever she could, looking radiant and proud.

2 Marshall, Joyce, Adams, Davies and Michell with Mrs Shackleton and Raymond Shackleton. Emily brought the children to welcome their father home from the Furthest South. It was the first time Raymond and Cecily had seen their father in two years.

3 In the three years after his return from *Nimrod*, Shackleton gave hundreds of lectures, travelling all over Europe. In 1910 he made a tour to the United States, accompanied by Emily, where he met Peary, the man who claimed to have discovered the North Pole.

1

TOWN HALL, BURTON-ON-TRENT

THE BURTON-ON-TRENT MUNICIPAL OFFICERS' GUILD
has arranged with THE LECTURE AGENCY, Ltd., of London, for

SIR ERNEST

SHACKLETON

C.V.O., F.R.G.S.

TO GIVE HIS

LECTURE

ENTITLED:

"THE SOUTH POLE"

PHOTO BY THOMSON, NEW BOND STREET.

THURSDAY, NOV. 21 at 8

In addition to giving a popular account of his own South Polar Expedition, Sir Ernest will describe and explain the Expeditions under Capt. Scott and Capt. Amundsen.

The Lecture will be fully illustrated from PHOTOGRAPHS and some very striking KINEMATOGRAPH FILMS taken during the Expedition.

THE CHAIR WILL BE TAKEN BY

GEORGE T. LYNAM, Esq., M. Inst. C.E.

(President of the Guild.)

RESERVED SEATS, 3/- (Family Tickets to admit four), 10/6 ; UNRESERVED, 2/- & 1/-

Early Doors open at 7.30 p.m. for Ticket-holders only.　Ordinary Doors open at 7.40.　Carriages at 9.45 p.m.

PLAN OF HALL & Tickets now ready at HORNE, THOMPSON, & Co.'s Music Warehouse, 184 & 185 Station St., Burton-on-Trent, Telephone No. 471.　Tickets may also be had from members of the Guild, or from
TOWN HALL, BURTON-ON-TRENT.　　　　WAUDE THOMPSON, *Guild Hon. Secretary.*

Late Cars will be run to Ashby

1 In addition to making speeches, Shackleton was invited to model polar clothing for Burberry's. The company was the leading light in the development of polar clothing and named jackets and boots after Shackleton. A Shackleton jacket was recommended to the British Mount Everest expedition members in the 1920s.

2 Raymond and Cecily Shackleton accompanied their father and mother on one leg of Shackleton's European lecture tour, travelling to several cities including Copenhagen.

3 Shackleton was always popular with women, with his charming smile and his buccaneering manner. Here he is photographed in Mrs Denton's garden on 22 July 1914.

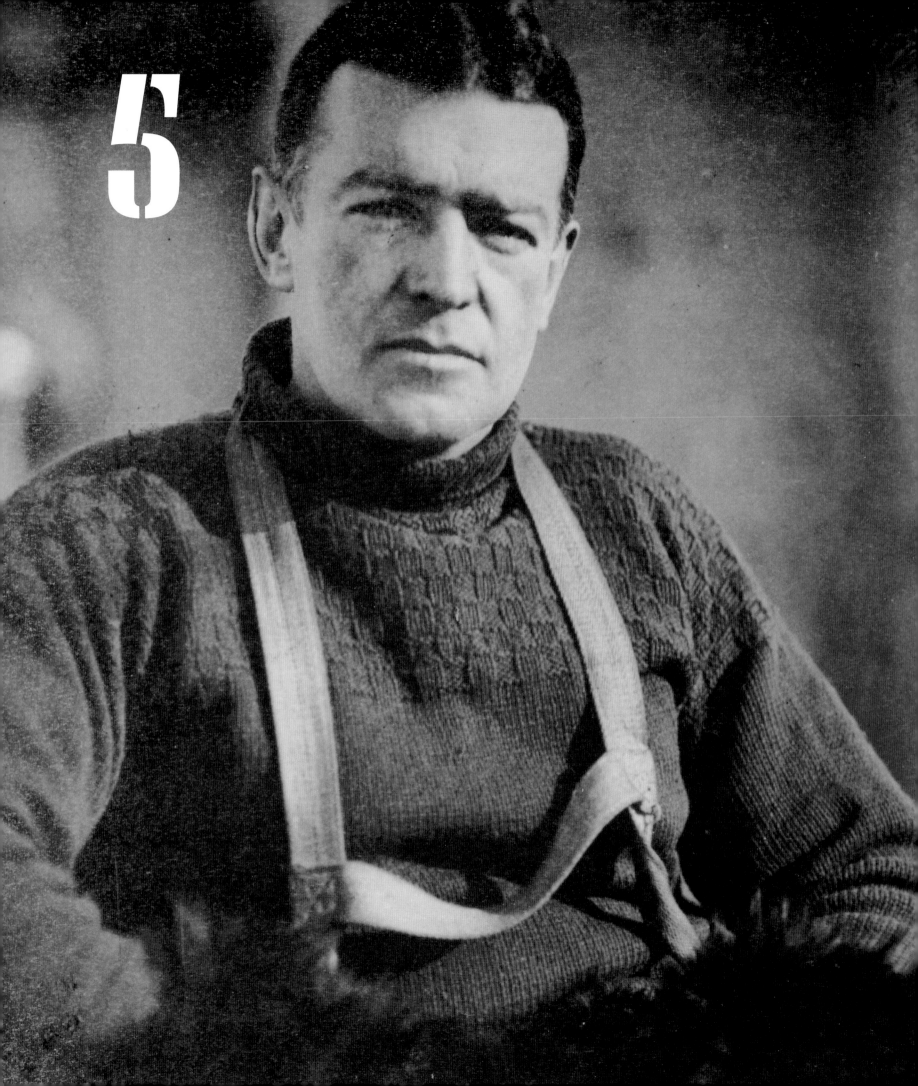

5

ENDURANCE AND THE AURORA RELIEF EXPEDITION 1914-17

Opposite: Sir Ernest Shackleton photographed by Hurley in 1915.
Right: The map of the Antarctic continent, published in The Imperial Trans-Antarctic Expedition in 1914, shows the proposed route from the Weddell Sea across to the Ross Sea. This copy was presented to Percy Illingworth, who, having served as Junior Lord of the Treasury, helped raise funds for this expedition.

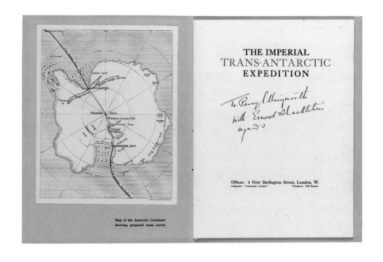

At the threshold of the new year, 1914, Shackleton publicly announced his new expedition. The Scott debacle was now playing into his hands. After the morbid wallowing in glorious death came a reaction of injured pride at having lost the race for the South Pole. The crossing of Antarctica, it was thought, would re-establish British prestige in polar exploration, and hence national supremacy in general.

The Government had promised Shackleton a grant of £10,000, on condition that he match it privately. Money he had none, nor did he invite financial trust. He was still burdened by debt. A late repayment had made an unforgiving enemy of William Beardmore, his erstwhile patron of the *Nimrod* expedition. Deserted by most of his wealthy supporters, he had to start all over again. He simply applied a talent for obliterating awkward aspects of the past and making influential friends to construct a new circle of appropriate contacts. From Amundsen he obtained a reluctant cable of endorsement. He wheedled funds out of rich and normally cautious people. His sheer force of character, leavened by good humour, gave him an overriding power to persuade. The culmination came at the end of June. Unexpectedly, a Dundee millionaire, Sir James Caird, gave Shackleton, through sheer admiration of his resistance to adversity, a munificent £24,000. This finally secured the enterprise.

Shackleton wanted absolutely to get away during that summer of 1914. He was being swept along on a wave of activity on which he always thrived. His palpable hurry gave his donors no time for second thoughts. It was just as well. His plan was an essay in systemic optimism. With little time to prepare, he proposed starting from the Weddell Sea and, via the familiar Beardmore Glacier, finishing at McMurdo Sound. The only trouble was that the Weddell Sea was little known, but manifestly treacherous, and no one had actually landed on the southern coast, where Shackleton proposed to go ashore.

His first need was a ship. Insolvent as he was, before Sir James Caird arrived on the scene, he yet made one materialise. It was a fairly straightforward act of credit and persuasion. There was in Norway a wooden ship, called *Polaris*, strengthened for the ice. She was a sailing ship of 300 tons, barquentine rigged, with auxiliary power, and specially built for Arctic cruises. That scheme had failed, and *Polaris* was decanted onto the market. Luckily for Shackleton, the demand had collapsed. Without money first actually changing hands, he acquired the ship, and in June 1914 she arrived in the Thames. Shackleton changed her name to *Endurance*. This was from his family motto, *Fortitudine vincimus*: 'By endurance we conquer'. Compared to *Nimrod* she was at least new but did not handle as well in a seaway.

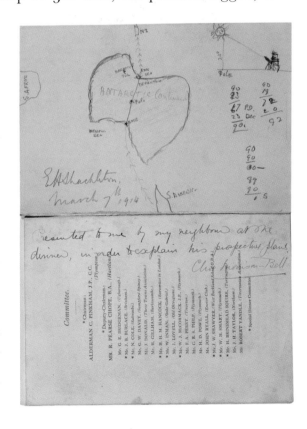

Endurance sailed down the Thames, roughly as intended, on the first day of the fateful August 1914. Soon after, on the fourth of the month, Britain declared war on Germany. The First World War was under way. After some doubt, and on the advice of various people from the King downwards, Shackleton decided to carry on. For one thing, it was generally thought that the war would finish after a short, sharp campaign, 'home by Christmas', so there would be no point in staying in England simply in the expectation of being sent out to fight.

Shackleton was not actually on board *Endurance* as she pitched and tossed down the Atlantic. He remained behind to settle various difficulties. Because of his affair with Rosalind Chetwynd, amongst other things, his marriage was under strain, and he had to make his peace with Emily. Eventually, late in September, he left England on a mailboat, and caught up with *Endurance* at Buenos Aires in the middle of October. On the twenty-sixth of the month, he finally sailed.

Endurance, low and black like *Nimrod*, made her way out into the ocean, with land sinking astern, Antarctic bound at last. In the isolation of a ship at sea, its world bounded by the horizon, Shackleton got the measure of his men, and they of him. One thing yet again quickly became apparent. Shackleton afloat was more impressive than Shackleton ashore. Released from the constraints of an uncongenial existence, he was at least once more in his element, a seaman on the deck of his ship, happy only when the shore dissolved into the distance. He was a privateer sailing out yet again in search of fame and fortune.

As on *Nimrod*, many on board, like Shackleton himself, were outcasts of a kind. There was, for example, the ship's Captain, a wayward New Zealander called Frank Worsley. The expedition doctors, Alexander Macklin and James McIlroy, were restless wanderers too. There was a classic misfit in the person of Thomas Hans Orde-Lees, a Captain in the Royal Marines, where he was baited for his unconventionality. In a similar mould was that vital figure of the age of sail, the ship's carpenter – 'Chips' or 'Chippy' in mariner's argot – Harry McNeish, a cantankerous Scot from Dundee. Rather more likeable, but in the same category, were two men who had followed Shackleton from the *Nimrod* expedition. One was the artist, George Marston, the other, now second in command, a member of the quartet who had stood at the Furthest South in 1909, Frank Wild.

King Edward Cove, South Georgia, 1914. Endurance *is the smaller of the two ships at anchor. Shackleton had intended staying in South Georgia only for a few days but in the event they were there for several weeks. He felt comfortable there, amongst the whalers, safe, at last, from his creditors.*

By now, Wild was wholly Shackleton's man, all earlier doubts forgotten. This change of heart had its origins in the return from the Furthest South in 1909. Wild was suffering the agonies of dysentery, in sore need of farinaceous food. Supplies were still failing. One day Shackleton forced on him his own single breakfast biscuit. The effect on Wild was as if no one had ever been so kind to him before. He had accepted that he did not belong within civilisation, and sought the wastes beyond. The born second in command, he had long been in search of a leader to whom he could attach himself, and in Shackleton on the polar trail, he had found one.

Not quite a typical seaman, nor at home on land, Wild did not really have much in common with most of the others on board. In fact, the whole party seemed a product of random choice. There had been a grotesquely mixed bag of five thousand applicants and Shackleton's method of selection was impenetrable. By a kind of poetic justice, there was now even a stowaway. He was a young Welshman called Percy Blackborrow, who had been smuggled aboard at Buenos Aires by accomplices who felt the ship was undermanned. Accepting the dictates of chance, Shackleton duly signed him on.

On 5 November, after an easy passage, *Endurance* made her landfall under the saw-tooth, ice-capped peaks of South Georgia and anchored in the shelter of the fjord at Grytviken. Although on a British colony, this was a Norwegian whaling station. The whalers were surprised to see Shackleton but he was glad to see them. He had to complete his supplies, financial disarray having dogged him to the last. Once again, he had run out of money.

To Shackleton, the great attraction of South Georgia was that it had remained truly an island. It still had neither cable nor radio, and was therefore completely cut off from the outside world. There was thus no instant way of referring back to check his financial standing. The whaling managers, with a touch of the pirate in themselves, recognised it in others. Shackleton needed all his powers of persuasion to overcome their caution, but overcome it he did. He acquired what he wanted on credit, which he needed most of all.

From another point of view, the whalers were confounded by Shackleton's casual planning. They, after all, knew the waters best of all. They reinforced the warnings given to Shackleton in England about the

Frank Hurley was the ultimate photographer who would go to any lengths to take a good picture. More than once he hauled himself and his equipment high up above the decks in order to frame just the image he required.

dangers of the Weddell Sea, with its imperfectly charted coast, and its slow, remorseless, whirling ice. They also doubted whether *Endurance* was built for the task ahead. Shackleton, the invincible optimist, brushed aside such reasoned advice. He did, however, listen to reports that it was the worst ice season within living memory. He decided to wait until the southern summer was more advanced.

So it was only after a full month had passed that, on 5 December, *Endurance* finally left South Georgia. She found the pack ice before 60° South, well short of the Antarctic Circle, some 400 miles away and ominously far north. To begin with, however, *Endurance* sailed easily through open leads along the eastern coast of the Weddell Sea, discovering new land along the way. Shackleton began making plans to go ashore. This was to be at Vahsel Bay, at the southeast corner of the Weddell Sea. It had only been discovered a few years earlier by a German expedition under Wilhelm Filchner – who himself had narrowly escaped disaster. He had only sighted the place but never actually landed.

The same fate hovered over Shackleton. On 19 January 1915, *Endurance* was beset. Now it was not men, but the ice that was in command. On 20 February, in the grip of tight-packed floes, *Endurance* swept past Vahsel Bay, still far off on the horizon. Shortly afterwards, she began drifting north. A few weeks later, the shore had disappeared, and there was no question of being carried back. By the middle of March, it was clear that there was to be no landing after all. That was Shackleton's greatest stroke of luck. On most counts, he was monumentally unqualified for what he had set out to achieve. Had he gone ashore, his fate would have been sealed. Now, in the frozen half-world between land and sea, an element more familiar, he had a chance to survive.

In the light of later knowledge, his choice of route and direction was in fact logical. By doing it in reverse, at it were, he avoided the enervating climb of the usual route. Starting from the Weddell Sea meant a gradual rise to the summit of the polar plateau, and then a quick descent down the escarpment on the other side. It is the usual path of adventurers today. At the time, however, the terrain as far as the Pole was quite unknown. Nobody had been there yet. The crossing was in all 1,500 miles. Shackleton blithely thought to cover the distance in a hundred days. That meant a daily run of fifteen miles, with no margin for setbacks of any kind. The assumptions bordered on the

feckless. Amundsen, after all, the finest traveller of them all, had only averaged sixteen miles a day on his conquest of the Pole.

Technically, Shackleton was still far behind and ill prepared. At least Amundsen had persuaded him that skis and dogs were the key to travel in the snow. Abandoning his bizarre trust in horses, Shackleton had now taken dogs, one hundred to begin with – but no one knew how to drive them. Likewise, he had taken skis, but of the twenty-eight men on board, Orde-Lees was the only one with any skill – and he was not marked for the transcontinental journey. Shackleton's own preparation had been a few days in 1914 at Finse, the Norwegian ski resort. There, for the first time since struggling back from the Furthest South under Scott in 1903, he once more tried to ski, but without much faith and, despite Amundsen's urging, he yet again discarded the ski as the instrument of polar travel. There had also been desultory trials of motor sledges, which turned out to be useless in the field.

Shackleton's plans for getting home were equally unconsidered. He had arranged for a second party to land at McMurdo Sound and lay depots for him on the other side of the continent. Their expedition ship was *Aurora*. She belonged to Douglas Mawson, the Australian who had reached the South Magnetic Pole under Shackleton in 1909 and had returned to Antarctica on an expedition of his own. By cable, and at a very modest price, he let Shackleton have the ship. Shackleton's preparations, however, had been harum-scarum. He had in fact no money for *Aurora* or indeed her crew. She was waiting at Hobart in Australia, and so he simply counted on the generosity of Australians to see him through.

Above all, there remained the nagging doubt over Shackleton's health. Others, and inwardly he himself, knew that high altitude was his bane. In civilisation, he had blithely made his plan seem sensible. Now, he was perhaps not so sure. He was in fact not really fit. At home he took no exercise. In Buenos Aires he was ill. It might have been a heart attack. The doctors did not really know, because Shackleton was still a reluctant patient and never let them near him to find out.

When the die was cast and *Endurance* was inexorably drifting north, the transantarctic crossing dissolved into a dream. Shackleton in one way was relieved. One set of uncertainties was lifted from his head. He betrayed no open regrets for what might have been. From the embers of one ambition, he plucked another. He would get everyone back alive. With danger as his inspiration, now Shackleton really came into his own. He was the born leader of a forlorn hope.

Shackleton had to deal with the strains of isolation. *Endurance* did have radio, but for some reason it did not work. The world was out of reach. His first task was to weld the men under him into a single body. They fell into four groups, mutually incompatible. To start with, Shackleton had a deep psychological need for someone who unquestioningly submitted to him, and was an invincible optimist into the bargain. Two men played that part. One was Frank Wild, the other the diminutive, sometimes egregious Leonard Hussey, a sometime archaeologist who had been on excavations in Africa and imperfectly played the banjo. This last accomplishment, Shackleton thought, would be good for morale.

Then there was the ship's crew, a closed society of professional seamen. Originally, they had signed on for a single voyage, so that after landing the shore party, they would return to port. At the last moment, Shackleton had decided to keep *Endurance* for the winter in the ice. As it turned out, he would have had to do that anyway, but the change of mind lingered as a threat to morale.

Next, and curiously out of place, were three scientists. They were a necessary evil. Shackleton only took them because promoting the expedition required a sop to higher moral purpose. There was a biologist, James Clark, a geologist called James Wordie, and Reginald James, a physicist. James, a product of the Cavendish Laboratory at Cambridge, was by far the most original, doing early work in X-ray crystallography. They all brought their ivory towers with them, but behind his bespectacled bland exterior, James had an appreciation of human nature and a quiet sense of humour that appealed to all.

Finally, there was the intended transcontinental party. This was a kind of elite in which was concentrated polar experience. The nucleus consisted of Shackleton himself, together with Wild and Marston. Macklin was also included, together with an Australian called Frank Hurley and Tom Crean, an Irish Royal Navy petty officer. All, except Macklin, had been south before. Crean had been on both of Scott's expeditions. Hurley had been to the Antarctic with Mawson. So too, incidentally, had Wild.

Another compulsive wanderer, Hurley was a highly talented photographer and film cameraman. It was to him that Shackleton largely owed the existence of the expedition, having played on the picture and film rights. Hurley was not popular, being abrasive and irrepressible in manner, individualistic and unwilling to conform to the dictates of the group. He was, however, practical, resourceful and tough. Not quite submitting to Shackleton's authority, Hurley was the one man of whom Shackleton stood a little in awe.

Such was the ill-assorted company at Shackleton's disposal. Here he began truly demonstrating his leadership. Although he had his favourites, he did not give the appearance of having cronies. He walked alone. He somehow counteracted the fragmentation into cliques, and the chronic irritation at seeing the same faces that are the penalties of groups in isolation. Except for a few incorrigible malcontents, he made each man feel equally important. Tellingly, his nickname was now quite simply 'the Boss'. It had been coined by Wild on the *Nimrod* expedition – at first not wholly in admiration. Now it stuck.

As the winter night wore on, the endless broken plain of luminescent ice swirled northwards with *Endurance* helpless in its grip, like a plaything of the Fates. Subjected to the eerie dance of the Aurora Australis – the southern lights – Shackleton and his men were in limbo. The return of the sun on 26 July was the harbinger of spring, the cruel season here, as elsewhere. The ice began to stir. The floe cradling *Endurance* cracked, exposing her to the pressure of the pack. As the whalers on South Georgia had warned, her lines were all wrong. She had an overhanging stern counter. Her hull sloped inwards from the bilges. Both meant that the ice could get a grip. After various shocks, by rumbling, rafting floes, like an earthquake in the crust floating on the sea, *Endurance* was finally crushed. The date was 27 October 1915. Shackleton and his men were now shipwrecked mariners, marooned on the ice. Since becoming beset, *Endurance* had drifted 1,300 miles, and made about seven degrees of latitude to the north, homewards as it were.

The qualities of leadership are rarely comfortable. Especially in civilisation, Shackleton could be ruthless and truculent. Few of his men actually liked him. But now, in this crisis, he radiated a kind of brute, comforting force. Hopeless as they seemed, marooned on a frozen sea, they believed he would get them home. He had said so in those words. He was determined to survive and instilled that hope in his subordinates. The heart of the matter was that he really cared for the lives of the motley crowd that he

had assembled, even the less likeable, if not the crowd itself. He felt that he had to repay the trust they had shown in putting their lives in his hands.

Their state of mind was his first concern. Men suddenly deprived of their points of reference are faced with a mental vacuum. The leader has to provide stimulation to prevent collapse. After abandoning ship, Shackleton ordered an immediate march westwards towards the nearest known land, in the Antarctic peninsula. It was futile from the start. The central loads were two heavy lifeboats on sledges. Men floundered and hauled on foot in mushy snow over a tumbled chaos of rafted ice. Even the dogs had to relay their laden sledges. It was activity for its own sake, designed to prevent the collapse of morale that doing nothing would have entailed. After a few days, and a pitiful few backbreaking miles Shackleton abandoned the march on 1 November. By then, the sheer grinding toil had cured the numbness of the original shock.

Shackleton now stopped on a solid-looking floe among the confusion, and settled down to wait, while wind and current did their work. The place was called Ocean Camp. In one way, it was a repository of the might have been. On the march Orde-Lees, that therapeutic figure within the group, the scapegoat now an outcast among outcasts, had skied effortlessly back and forth along the straggling procession to maintain communication. Too late, he had finally convinced Shackleton of the role that skis could have played in the crossing of the continent.

What is more, the tents now nestling on the floe were an innovation. They were of the dome type, designed by Shackleton and Marston, and originally tested at Finse, before sailing. They were stable, storm-proof, years ahead of their time, and the precursors of the modern type. In diet, too, Shackleton was a forerunner. The boxes of sledging rations stacked around the floe contained dehydrated food – a new technology, applied to exploration for the first time. Moreover, he was at odds with the doctors in his acceptance of the theory of vitamins, especially in the prevention of scurvy. There again, he was a precursor. The theory had only been published in 1912.

Shackleton believed in the flash of inspiration. He was less at home with methodical preparation. He had not, for example, organised the abandonment of the ship with proper foresight, so that now there

Early on the morning of 28 October 1915, after their first night camped on the floe, Shackleton, Wild and Hurley returned to the wreck of Endurance, *retrieving several tins of benzine. Once a fire was kindled at 'Dump Camp' breakfast was cooked. Wild served it to the men in their sleeping bags, later writing, 'they did not fully appreciate the effort that went into preparing or serving the meal'.*

were dreary trudges over the snow to salvage what had been left behind. Hurley, in particular, fetched his negatives, surprisingly not considered worth saving in the first wave of disaster, but now the only pictorial record of what had happened.

For nearly a month, the wreck of *Endurance* was cradled by the ice that destroyed her, and the sight of her derelict remains were at least a thread of connection with the world. Then on 21 November, she finally sank, swallowed by the swirling floes and the remorseless sea beneath. This was the final shock. Now the men on the ice were in greater danger of apathy and despair. There was nothing to do but wait.

This necessity for waiting in patience called for everything that Shackleton was not. Yet somehow he controlled the restlessness within. He stalked the camp, radiating a singular force that, without words, supported his companions and, excepting one or two unbalanced individuals, prevented their mental collapse. The reverse side of this self-control, exacerbated by inaction, was an overpowering moodiness, which put his men on edge.

On 21 December, a month after *Endurance* disappeared beneath the ice, Shackleton announced another march to land. Inaction was telling on the sanity of some of the party, and he was worried by dissatisfaction and suicidal tendencies among the seamen. Through activity, and the sense of doing something to help themselves, he hoped to halt the slide into mental disintegration. So, on 23 December, for the second time, the caravan started out westwards towards the Antarctic peninsula. It was far worse than before. The illusion of solid going underfoot was shattered. It was the summer solstice, and the snow was of the mushy kind. The pack was fragmenting into chaotic working floes, open leads and shifting icebergs. Merely hauling the lifeboats on the distorted sledges over pressure ridges, tangled hummocks and thin ice that broke under the runners was torture laced with fear.

The inevitable moment of mutiny came on 27 December, when McNeish, the carpenter, refused to obey orders and stopped work. He considered it futile. Under the circumstances, Shackleton had only force of character to impose his will. He was not called 'the Boss' for nothing. The trouble was that McNeish was simply giving vent to general dissatisfaction. Shackleton dealt with the situation by reading out ship's articles, and declaring that they were not terminated by the sinking of the ship according to the letter of the law but continued until they returned to port. That satisfied the lower deck. McNeish, personally, he dealt with by threatening to shoot him unless he obeyed orders. That settled the affair.

Outside circumstances also played a part. The way ahead was blocked by shifting floes and opening leads. Next day, Shackleton ordered a retreat to the safest looking floe, and there once more he decided to wait upon events. He called this Patience Camp. It was a very few miles west of Ocean Camp, the place from which he had set off. This had been more than an exercise in futility. Shackleton had had obscure premonitions of disaster. Worsley, master navigator that he was, helped by James, used to handling instruments, had been minutely charting the course of Ocean Camp. After long moving directly north, it had lurched worryingly to the east. That threatened a course straight out of the Weddell Sea into the ocean beyond and a certain end. These waters were then unknown, but Shackleton sensed, what was later discovered, that hereabouts the currents divided. Not far to the west there was a branch that swept close to land, and therefore offered a glimmer of hope. Perhaps Shackleton's apparently irrational proceeding, by catching this western current, had tipped the scales towards survival.

He could only wait now, at the mercy of the sea and the slowly disintegrating ice. New Year 1916 came and went. The months passed. Shackleton again became noticeably moody and irritable. Still his odd personal magnetism held the party together and, in the midst of stagnation, kept despair at bay. They were running out of food, but this was almost by design. Since leaving the ship, they had been living on seals, to avoid making inroads into the original sledging rations. Orde-Lees in particular had wanted to slaughter large numbers to build up a reserve. Shackleton, angrily, declined. He had a better understanding of the British sailor's psychology. They were improvident, living for the day. To lay in stocks would persuade them that there was danger ahead and threaten their sanity. Starvation, on the whole, was preferable to madness.

As it was, ennui took hold. Worsley was perturbed that Shackleton had only brought two boats. This would not be enough when, inevitably, they had to take to the water. At the beginning of February, Shackleton agreed to fetch the third boat left behind at Ocean Camp, now brought within reach by the gyrating of the pack. It was just as well.

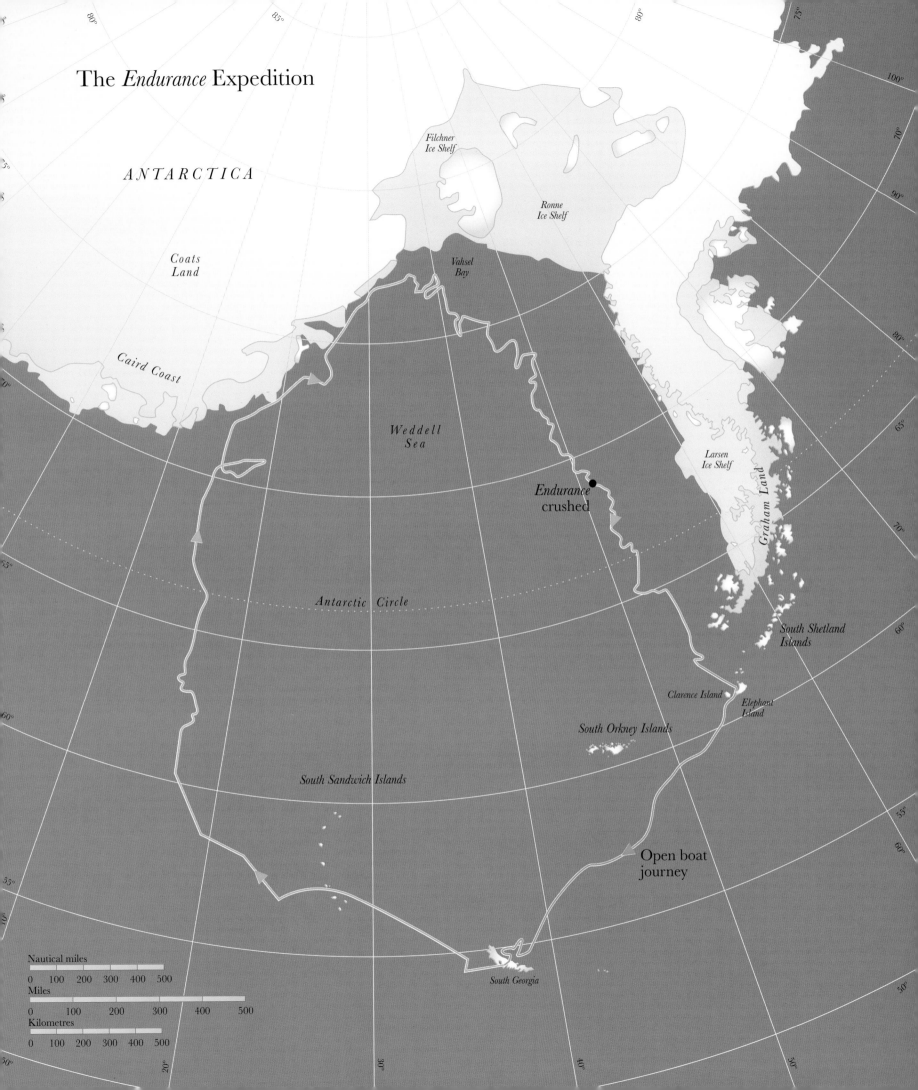

The *Endurance* Expedition

ANTARCTICA

*Filchner
Ice Shelf*

*Ronne
Ice Shelf*

*Coats
Land*

*Vahsel
Bay*

Caird Coast

*Weddell
Sea*

*Larsen
Ice Shelf*

Endurance
crushed

Graham Land

Antarctic Circle

*South Shetland
Islands*

Clarence Island

*Elephant
Island*

South Orkney Islands

Open boat
journey

South Sandwich Islands

South Georgia

Nautical miles

| 0 | 100 | 200 | 300 | 400 | 500 |

Miles

| 0 | 100 | 200 | 300 | 400 | 500 |

Kilometres

| 0 | 100 | 200 | 300 | 400 | 500 |

Thursday 23 March – almost the southern autumnal equinox – was a fateful day. The castaways had their first glimpse of land for sixteen months. Their floe had brought them within reach of Joinville Island, at the entrance to the Weddell Sea. Open leads ran enticingly in the right direction, suggesting a quick row ashore. Shackleton withstood the temptation, since he understood the trap of ice that would not bear, nor open enough to navigate. Within sight of land, he decided to remain on the ice. It was another epic decision, comparable to that moment seven years before, when Shackleton had turned back with the South Pole within reach.

The sight of land receding, so near and yet so far, almost broke some of the men. They were now on a melting floe, being swept out by a remorseless current into the open sea. At least it was in the vicinity of a scattered archipelago of off-shore islands. At the end of March, Shackleton ordered the surviving dogs to be shot. The others had been put down in stages before as their usefulness declined – also, incidentally, 'Mrs Chippy', McNeish's pet cat, with untold consequences for his embittered soul. The moment of taking to the sea was approaching. At least the dank fog and drizzle lifted, and April began with clear weather, which dissipated some of the gloom on the floe. Surrounded by open water, narrowing and widening as other shifting floes pulsated all around, Patience Camp was now heaving to an ocean swell, disconcertingly breaking up, to the enervating rasp of ice grinding against ice. At last, on 9 April, Shackleton ordered everyone into the boats. After five months in the alien half-world of the pack ice, Shackleton was in open water, his familiar element, once more.

For the next week the sad flotilla of three boats drove northwards, in a nightmare journey, sometimes under sail, sometimes rowed, subject to every diabolical caprice known to wind and sea and scattered ice. They were heading for Elephant Island, the outermost skerry of the coastal archipelago. Underlying all was the terror of missing the landfall and being driven helplessly into the implacable ocean and the certainty of extinction. On the seventh day, somehow, against wind and tide, they reached their goal. By then, cold, fatigue, exhaustion, exposure and mental strain had told. Some had collapsed in the boats; others had lost their reason, temporarily at least. Shackleton and Wild had preserved a semblance of normality. Green, the cook, recovered as soon as he landed. He now had a familiar job, that of feeding his companions.

The first landing revealed a death trap. Tide marks showed that it was periodically submerged. Having scouted for a safer haven, Shackleton decided on one a few miles westwards along the northern coast. On 17 April, after a short stormy passage through offshore squalls, the three lifeboats arrived at the castaways' new home. Hospitable it was not. Elephant Island – named after the elephant seals that were once supposed to have flourished there – was a half-drowned barren peak of ice-capped rock. The refuge was a desolate spit of land underneath a glacier, but at least it was high enough out of the water not to be awash even in the worst of storms and highest tides. Above all it was, at last, *terra firma*. It was also utterly isolated and away from all shipping lanes. It might just as well have been another planet floating out in space.

Shackleton had made the first known landing on Elephant Island since American sealers in the 1830s. Even whalers never touched there now. Nor was a search expedition likely to try the island either. To wait for rescue was therefore out of the question. The marooned party would have to help themselves. Or rather, Shackleton would have to save them. By now, the Boss had acquired a true mythic quality. Always somehow apart, he was believed by everyone around him to be capable of making everything all right in the end. Flawed he might be, but he was the figure in which the dirty, exhausted, wild-eyed scarecrows on the beach could put their faith and hence cling to a vestige of sanity.

Shackleton decided that the only way out was immediately to sail to civilisation. That meant, in practice, heading for South Georgia. Cape Horn and the Falklands were closer, but they were to windward, which probably meant disaster. South Georgia was 700 miles away, and to leeward, which meant running before the prevailing winds, and hence having a better chance.

It was still the counsel of despair. It would have to be an open boat journey. At his disposal, Shackleton had the trio of lifeboats that had brought him thus far. They had all been named, incidentally: *Stancomb-Wills*, *Dudley Docker* and *James Caird*, after patrons of the expedition. (The first was named after Janet Stancomb-Wills, a wealthy spinster, who had chastely fallen for Shackleton's charm. Dudley Docker was a Birmingham industrialist who had recognised in Shackleton a manipulator of people like himself.) To take all boats and all twenty-eight men would have meant the end of all. Shackleton proposed sailing out in one boat with a small crew to fetch help. For his craft, he chose the *James Caird* – all of twenty-two feet overall and six feet on the beam – as the most seaworthy.

Broadly speaking, the same applied to the men. And so, on 24 April, a week after arriving on Elephant Island, Shackleton sailed off with five companions. Behind him, waving wanly on the beach, he left twenty-two men to wait in hope. Their leader was Frank Wild. Shackleton himself was perversely in a state of exultation. He had always wanted to make a great open boat journey. In fact, originally he had planned his attempt on the South Pole in 1908 as a crossing of the continent, dragging a portable boat in which he proposed sailing back to civilisation. The thought was barely sane, but at least now he had the chance of achieving this one ambition.

Frank Worsley shared that aim. He was on board as a gifted small boat handler; but above all as navigator. The whole journey depended on finding a spot in the ocean 700 miles off. It was rather like the proverbial search for a needle in a haystack. In the days before satellites and computerised global positioning, navigation depended on taking sights of heavenly bodies, laborious calculation and looking up tables. It needed precise time, which in this case was doubtful, besides certainty over the vessel's behaviour, which was more doubtful still. The *James Caird*, with round bilges and no keel, made monumental leeway, which could only be estimated. Navigation was not only a question of arithmetic, it was an art, linked with a vein of inspired guesswork. There would be no second chance. If they missed their landfall, they could not turn round and beat back against the wind. They would be swallowed up by the unforgiving sea.

By comparison, the task of keeping afloat was almost secondary. That was in the hands of McNeish, the shipwright, and third member of the crew. Unpleasant he might be, but he was a true craftsman and, like Shackleton, inspired absolute trust. It was he who had made the boat ready for sea. Swooping in trough and over the crest of the violent waves, she might have risked breaking her back. McNeish had prevented that by reinforcing her with a mast from one of the other boats laid inside along the bilge. On the ice, he had already raised the freeboard and covered the poop. On Elephant Island, he had improvised the remainder of the deck with wood from a sledge and some canvas. So strictly speaking, the *James Caird* was no longer an open boat.

This original photograph of Endurance *was brought from Elephant Island in the small open boat by Shackleton and is captioned in his own handwriting.*

The original photograph of "The Endurance." brought from Elephant Island in the small open boat by Sir Ernest Shackleton

Shackleton first sailed north to escape the danger of ice. Then, after two days, he swung northeast to head for South Georgia. The *James Caird* now had the elements behind her. The prevailing wind was from the west. So too were the long southern rollers, which, together with the unceasing current of the Great Easterly Drift, encircled the globe. With all sails set, the boat drove before the wind. Making her passage was a relatively simple task of practised seamanship. That had dictated the choice of the remainder of the crew. Crean was one, Tim McCarthy, also Irish (but a merchant seaman), another and finally there was Vincent, physically the strongest of them all, but a bully, already disrated on that account from bosun on *Endurance*. True to type, he now collapsed mentally early in the voyage. He remained a passenger, leaving five men to work the boat.

Except for Vincent, they were all mentally as well as physically tough. They needed all their resistance, as the sea hurled its fury at them. Enduring the strain of the stormiest seas on earth was the real key to survival. Day after day, the tortured hull lurched, rolled, swooped, heaved and pitched. It was battered by rogue waves, raked from stem to stern, and lifted by the surge of the swell, which meant frantic pumping and bailing to stay afloat. All senses were affronted. Without waterproofs, the men were constantly wet and cold. Always there was the cacophony of the wind roaring and whining, the malevolent hiss of the sea, rattling squalls of rain and mist, the creak and groan of timbers able to survive no one knew how much longer. Various crises were overcome: being pooped by a giant rogue wave, becoming unstable and top heavy because of freezing spume.

It was, however, the moral element that really counted. Somehow the will to survive had to be maintained, and the routine of a ship at seas as well. This was hard to carry out in a cockleshell challenging the might of the ocean. Changing the watch was a caricature of the normal. It meant crawling, bent double, in and out with no headroom, while the watch below rested uneasily squirming among the ballast. Meals involved balancing a Primus stove on legs and arms like acrobats, and swallowing the food between lurches of the hull. Like a Homeric figure, Shackleton, by his mere presence, even in the worst moments, inspired hope and trust. Nonetheless, he could not know how much more the human spirit could bear in the everlasting helplessness of an empty sea.

On 7 May, a piece of kelp brought the first sign of change. Next morning, the first birds appeared, guaranteeing land in the offing. Mist and driving squalls of rain blocked the view. Around midday, through a rift in the weather, land suddenly appeared. It was a dark, hostile crag, but it was land. It was the fifteenth day at sea. Worsley had made his landfall, almost exactly as intended. A sense of indescribable gratitude and relief settled on the boat. It was only momentary. Every sailor knows that making land is more perilous than most trials out at sea. Shackleton grasped that some of the crew were on the verge of collapse, and he had no idea how much longer they could hold out.

At the critical moment, Nature, of course, then played another trick. A storm blew up, rose to hurricane force from the southwest, and began driving the *James Caird* ashore. It was every captain's nightmare. Shoaling waters brought confused, violent, tumultuous, choppy seas. For most of the night, they battered the weatherworn hull, more devastating in a way than anything in the long voyage so far. There was little searoom. Shipwreck in the last lap, after all, seemed to be their fate. They were saved by what hitherto had seemed an error of judgement by Shackleton.

Now, at the start, against Worsley's objections, he had obstinately insisted on a particular rig. It consisted of two masts, so spaced, and with such sails, that she griped to windward, so that steering all those hundreds of miles was a harsh countervailing struggle across the wind to keep her on course. That fault on the open sea was now her salvation. Worsley used it to make her claw her way up wind, and slowly move out of danger, only to be threatened from another quarter. At one point, the *James Caird* seemed about to run aground on Annenkov Island, offshore, but at the last moment was saved by a random eddy, and the wind providentially dropped.

She was able to continue her voyage but not for long. For one thing, she was on the south coast of the island, and the whaling stations, where rescue lay, were on the north. Her battered hull was in no state to make the passage round by sea. That also held for the crew. Exposure had taken its toll. Also, the strain of the voyage aside, they had run out of drinking water two days before. Finding some quickly was a matter of life and death. So Shackleton put into a nearby fjord called King Haakon Bay, and immediately stumbled on a stream of sweet fresh water. They dropped on their knees and slaked their choking thirst.

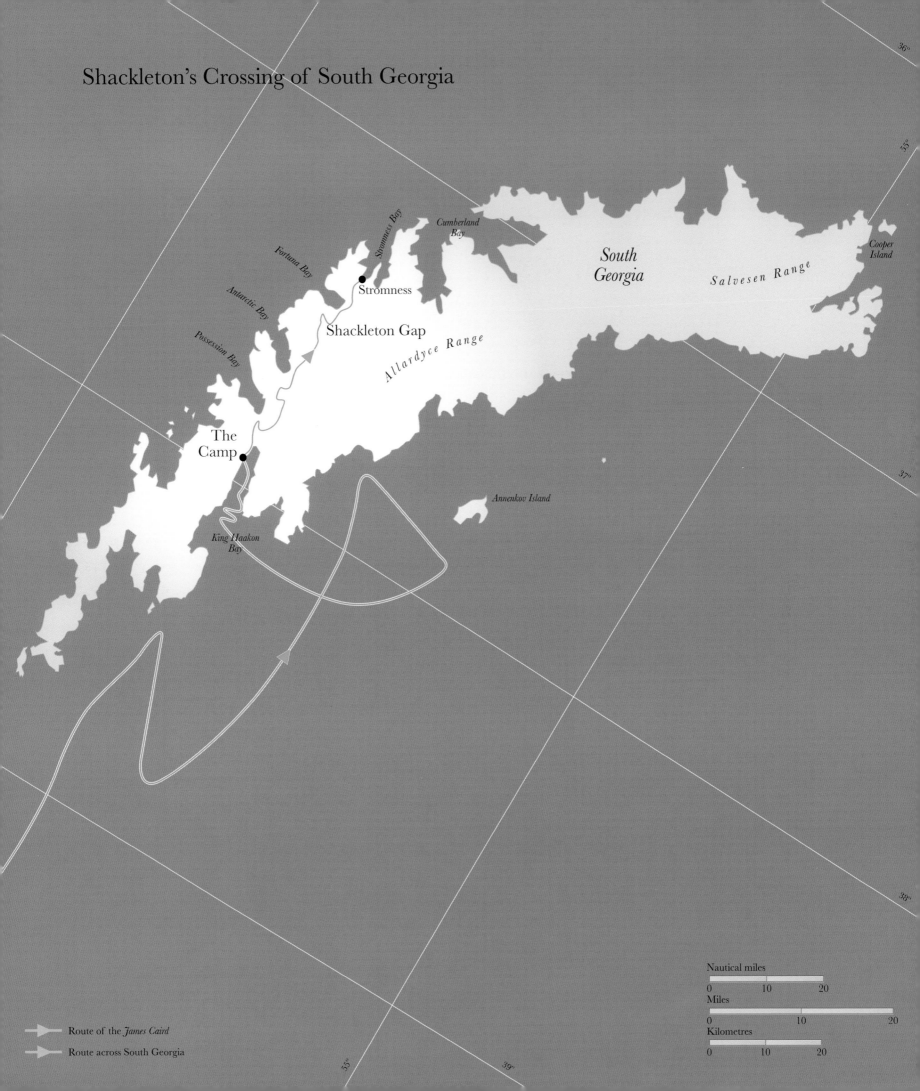

Shackleton's Crossing of South Georgia

Fortuna Bay

Stromness Bay

Cumberland Bay

South Georgia

Salvesen Range

Cooper Island

Antarctic Bay

Stromness

Shackleton Gap

Allardyce Range

Possession Bay

The Camp

Annenkov Island

King Haakon Bay

36°

55°

37°

38°

55°

39°

Nautical miles

0   10   20

Miles

0   10   20

Kilometres

0   10   20

→ Route of the *James Caird*

→ Route across South Georgia

The date was 10 May 1916. Seventeen days after leaving Elephant Island, their epic boat journey had come to an end.

After a few days' rest, Shackleton re-embarked, and had the boat rowed to the head of the fjord. There he made camp and settled McNeish, McCarthy and Vincent. All three were now at the end of their tether, with Vincent still in a state of mental collapse. Together with Worsley and Crean, Shackleton was going to embark on the only alternative left to him. He was simply going to cross South Georgia on foot and fetch help from the whalers.

What was in prospect was a traverse of about twenty miles along low mountains rising out of firm snowfields safely encasing glaciers, with an occasional ice slope in the way. To practised mountaineers, it would not have been much. But except for Worsley, they were not mountaineers. After the open boat journey, they were weakened by exposure and exhaustion. Their clothes were threadbare; their boots smooth-soled and therefore made for fatal slips. McNeish rectified this with screws cannibalised from the boat and his adze went along as an ice axe. Once more technicalities somehow faded. Both those going and those waiting behind depended absolutely on the faith they had long since blindly put in Shackleton.

It was a nightmare journey, with a sketchy map and much blundering in soft snow. They found passes with wrong turnings and had the demoralising task of having to regain lost height. To Shackleton, speed was the crux. Although right in the path of the westerlies, the weather was preternaturally calm. They had to cross while the going was good. Without tent or sleeping bag, one gale would have been fatal.

Shackleton took various risks, like glissading down an unknown slope. But time, not terrain, was the foe. Delay was the greater risk. Day turned to night, but Shackleton, in a state of controlled impatience, drove them all on continuously without sleep and with rests only to eat. Exhaustion passed through the state of pure fatigue into hallucination, shadows turning into ghosts. Then, at a certain point, in the distance, they heard the sound of a steam whistle. From the voyage out, they knew it was the call of the whalers to work. It was the first outside human sound since they had last been there, eighteen months before. It removed the grinding strain of feeling lost. Together with a landmark beyond a ridge, they now had their bearings. Somehow they staggered along the last lap, up a ridge, and at the end, with a reckless abseil down a frozen waterfall, they reached the Norwegian whaling station of Stromness. They had been travelling continuously for thirty-six hours without sleep.

With emaciated, filthy, ragged faces ingrained with blubber soot and eyes with a maniacal stare, the three castaways made their way to the house of the station manager. His name was Thoralf Sørlle. He had met Shackleton before; he did not recognise the figure before him now. Identity established, Sørlle forbore to remind Shackleton that he had predicted shipwreck from the start. He was only amazed at the tale of survival that was now being poured out. Shackleton was equally amazed at the news from the outside world relayed by Sørlle – admittedly not quite up to date, because South Georgia was still without radio or cable. This much, however, was clear. The war was still raging with millions falling on the battlefield, and new weapons of futuristic aspect like poison gas and aircraft.

The whalers were boundless in their admiration and generosity. Admittedly, Shackleton had got himself into a tight corner but, unlike most of his kind, had got himself out of it, so far. A whalecatcher quickly got up steam, and went round to fetch the men in King Haakon Bay, with Worsley as pilot. He found them all alive, and soon brought them back, together with the *James Caird*, the memento of their Homeric voyage.

Shackleton was desperately concerned about the men on Elephant Island. He had already been gone almost a month, and they would be anxiously expecting rescue. The whalers lent him a transport ship called *Southern Sky*, fully fitted out and complete with crew. On 23 May, he sailed in high hope, only to be stopped by ice, which, with a steel ship, he dared not challenge. In disappointment he sailed to the Falklands, which were closer than South Georgia and also the nearest cablehead. There, on 31 May 1916, he made his first contact with the outside world since leaving Buenos Aires in 1914.

The cables now filtering back and forth left Shackleton feeling that his achievement was unappreciated at home, and his enemies were biding their time. He made two more abortive attempts to rescue the men on Elephant Island. Meanwhile, the Admiralty in London decided to try bringing them out, using *Discovery* no less. Amiable they were not and understandably so. They were grappling with the aftermath of the Battle of Jutland and a depressing naval stalemate, which brought incalculable consequences in its train.

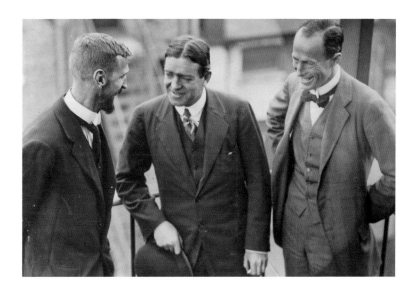

John King Davis, Shackleton and Douglas Mawson photographed after the Nimrod *expedition. Prior to* Endurance, *Mawson sold* Aurora *to Shackleton and it was this ship, captained by John King Davis, that was used to rescue the members of the Ross Sea party.*

Tense and irritable, and with his less agreeable shore-going self re-emerging, Shackleton was determined to rescue the men on Elephant Island by himself. Without money or credit, he somehow organised one more attempt. He sailed over to Punta Arenas, in the Straits of Magellan and, on the strength of his character and some affinity with the Chileans, he persuaded the authorities in Santiago to lend him a vessel. She was *Yelcho*, originally an ocean-going tug, and now a rusting mass of battered iron of some 150 tons, whose engines were in sorry disrepair. But she was a ship, and she was afloat. By 25 August, Shackleton, Crean and Worsley, who had instinctively stuck together since the crossing of South Georgia, were on board.

Shackleton's luck now turned. Wind, current and tide had driven the pack off. On 30 August, *Yelcho* sailed in open water along the coast of Elephant Island, and found the spit of land on which the men had been left. All twenty-two were still alive. That included Blackborrow, the stowaway, who had had several toes amputated because of gangrene following frostbite. The operation had been a feat in itself. It was carried out under primitive conditions in a dirty, dry-stone hut roofed with the two lifeboats left behind. Macklin was surgeon while McIlroy was anaesthetist. Sterilisation was minimal and there was only just enough chloroform to put the patient under. To the doctors' surprise, there were no complications.

The party was at the end of its tether, both physically and mentally. The fact that they had survived, was due to the quiet leadership of Frank Wild. He now literally worshipped Shackleton and through all the long unexpected wait, somehow kept up the belief that the Boss would see them through.

Shackleton himself was on the tender that ferried the men aboard, but as if afraid of tempting fate, he refused to set foot ashore. Within the hour, *Yelcho* was steaming out again. The ice kept its distance, and with no other impediment than the natural heaving of the grey-green sea, she made her way back to Punta Arenas, coming alongside on 3 September. Shackleton had escaped from the ice of the Weddell Sea, done the Open Boat Journey, then organised four separate rescue expeditions and saved his men, every one. At least he had accomplished one ambition out of the wreck of all his hopes. He had not lost a single man.

Shackleton had in fact carried out the greatest rescue in the wake of the greatest disaster in either the Arctic or the Antarctic. This was now his pride. The fact that his troubles were largely of his own making he somehow managed to ignore. He created the illusion of snatching victory out of defeat. But he had not reached the end yet.

There still remained the Ross Sea Party, and their ship *Aurora*. When, on *Endurance*, Shackleton had left the cablehead behind at Buenos Aires, *Aurora* was at Hobart, Tasmania, and still had not sailed. Consequently, at the time he had not known whether she had reached her destination, and hence whether those vital depots at the foot of the Beardmore Glacier would have been laid. From the start, therefore, he was by no means certain of getting across alive. The whole enterprise seemed clouded from the start in make-believe. Now, Shackleton learned that the other half of his enterprise had been overtaken by disaster too.

Aurora had safely reached McMurdo Sound but, in May 1915, broke her moorings, and was driven by a southwest gale out to sea. For nearly a year, she was beset in the drifting ice, finally reaching Port Chalmers in New Zealand at the beginning of April 1916 – about the same time as Shackleton was preparing to leave the pack ice on the way to Elephant Island. The worst part of the affair was that *Aurora* had left the shore party marooned, and taken most of their supplies with her. Now she was waiting in New Zealand for the southern summer in order to sail back and rescue those left behind.

Shackleton assumed that he would be in command. After a triumphal progress through Chile from Punta Arenas, he intended to return to England with his men from *Endurance*, and then sail back to New Zealand for the rescue at McMurdo Sound. Along the way, it turned out that the British, Australian and New Zealand governments had jointly agreed to organise and pay for the relief. Shackleton, having been blamed for the trouble, was definitely not wanted. He begged angrily to disagree. At Buenos Aires, he abruptly turned round, taking Worsley with him for companionship. On locally borrowed money, with occasional free tickets, he somehow got them both all the complicated way back to New Zealand, by train and boat via Valparaíso, Panama and New Orleans, culminating in a Pacific crossing from San Francisco. After nearly two months he arrived in New Zealand. He had taken his enemies by surprise. Against official

opposition, using his inimitable amalgam of charm and sheer force of character with the hint of menace underneath, he quickly made influential friends, and forced his way on board.

On 20 December, Shackleton sailed south once more on *Aurora*. He had had to leave Worsley behind, and he himself was not in command. He had signed on as a subordinate officer, but to him that did not matter. He felt responsible for the men left in the Antarctic, and now all he wanted was to be part of the rescue.

As soon as land dipped below the horizon, Shackleton underwent his usual transformation. *Aurora*'s Captain was John King Davis, who had been a mate on *Nimrod*, now far away in the lost world of the

Edwardian era. He willingly changed roles. Forgetting his disapproval of Shackleton's reckless incompetence in sending *Aurora* out ill prepared, he now forgave all and turned once again into a fervent admirer.

On 10 January 1917, after an uneventful voyage, *Aurora* reached McMurdo Sound. What Shackleton found was dreadful. Of the ten men originally marooned, only seven remained. They were pallid, wild-eyed and all too clearly in a state of mental and physical disintegration. In fact, they were in a far worse state than the men on Elephant Island. They also bore a resentment against Shackleton for leaving them in the lurch. Yet once again the mysterious force within him compelled their submission and seemed to cure most of their ills.

Like ghosts from the past, there was an eerie repetition of episodes from the *Nimrod* expedition. The depots had been laid as planned. As on the previous occasion, it was Ernest Joyce who had carried it out. The exploit had cost three lives, but this side of the *Endurance* expedition had achieved its stated goal. In other words, by definition it had been a success, while Shackleton himself on *Endurance* had presided over a failure. Again he faced the irony that his presence seemed a bane, and where he was not, there was no blight on the course of events.

Hardest for Shackleton to bear was that these men had lived in Scott's hut from his second expedition and had only carried out his tasks thanks to the supplies left by his old enemy. On 25 January *Aurora* at last headed north again and, with relief, Shackleton turned his back on the graveyard of all his ambition. Meanwhile, he had written out a document for the party, in which he took upon himself the burden of full responsibility for them and all their misfortunes, even though he had been thousands of miles away.

On 9 February, he arrived at Wellington, New Zealand, and was welcomed as a hero. Very different was the scene when, on 29 May 1917, he had returned to the drabness of wartime England. There his arrival was hardly noticed, his adventure overshadowed by a country mired down in a savage and lethal stalemate.

1 The Imperial Trans-Antarctic Expedition offices were located in Burlington Street in London. Here Shackleton received the details of the 5,000 applicants eager to join his enterprise.

2 Shackleton had permanent financial worries and spent a great deal of his time up to the departure of *Endurance* trying to find the appropriate funding. In the end he was partially successful when the Dundee jute magnate and friend of Winston Churchill, Sir James Caird, asked Shackleton to visit him. Caird was impressed by Shackleton's determination in the face of serious financial setbacks and after the visit sent him a note which read: 'I have pleasure in giving you my cheque for £24,000, without any conditions, in the hope that others may make their gifts for this Imperial journey also free of all conditions.'

3 Cheques signed by Shackleton to the *Endurance* expedition members, including Frank Wild, July 1914.

PAYMASTERS ADVANCES

MAJOR. SIR E. SHACKLETON (Station) Murmansk

No. G89181   London 20th Nov 1911

The Union of London & Smiths Bank *Limited*

FINSBURY CIRCUS BRANCH

SALISBURY HOUSE, LONDON WALL, E.C.

Pay Lady Shackleton or Order

Two hundred pounds

£200

This Cheque must be endorsed by the p...

No. 128/L.39688   London, 1st July 1914

Lloyds Bank Limited

ST JAMES'S STREET, S.W.

Pay Capt. F. A. Worsley   or Order

ONE PENNY

No. 128/L.39711   London, 9th July 1914

Lloyds Bank Limited

ST JAMES'S STREET, S.W.

Pay Frank Wild Esq   or Order

Forty four pounds /-

THE IMPERIAL TRANS-ANTARCTIC EXPEDITION.

£44-1-0   COMMANDER

SECRETARY.

3

Endurance, formerly named *Polaris*, was christened by Shackleton after his family motto, *Fortitudine vincimus* ('By endurance we conquer'). She cost £14,000 and had to be painted black in Buenos Aires so that she would stand out against the ice.

T. Hussey
Capt Worsley ship "Endurance"
Tom Crean cross country
Frank Wild 2nd in Command

1

1 The members of the Imperial Trans-Antarctic Expedition, plus Captain Mackintosh from the Ross Sea party, aboard *Endurance* in London. The photograph was from Shackleton's album and is annotated in his own hand. Tom Crean, standing next to Shackleton, made the crossing of South Georgia with Worsley and Shackleton after their open boat journey.

2 Emily Shackleton and her daughter Cecily saw *Endurance* leave the West India Dock on 1 August 1914. Shackleton himself did not sail with *Endurance* but caught her up in Buenos Aires, having taken the mail boat.

'As I stood . . . and looked over the calm sea and upwards to the great stars blazing in velvet sky my mind flew forward to the unknown ways and the lonely trails as yet awaiting the feet of men and I wondered how our little party now playing mouth organs, banjos and mandolines would work and fare in the long dark days to come; the fight will be good.'

From Shackleton's diary, on leaving Buenos Aires for South Georgia, 26 October 1914

Shackleton's expedition was made up of two parties: this group of men, headed for the Weddell Sea under his command, and a second group, which, under the leadership of Aeneas Mackintosh, started from the Ross Sea and set out to meet the Trans-Antarctic team.

1 The first pack ice appeared on 8 December 1914. Shackleton had been warned by the whalers of South Georgia that it was a particularly bad year for ice but even he had not expected to encounter it so far north. They had not yet crossed the 57th parallel.

2 Three days later, on 11 December, *Endurance* reached the pack in the Weddell Sea. This time it was not possible to circumvent it. She had to be put straight in. Hurley was ecstatic, photographing and cine-filming with bare head and hands whilst the others were well wrapped up in hats and gloves.

Previous page: On 4 January 1915 *Endurance* became jammed in the pack, but five days later it opened up again and they were able to set sail and make some progress. Here the ship is once again trapped in the ice, at the point where she was finally frozen in.

1 With *Endurance* well and truly beset, her crew worked tirelessly over the following days and weeks to free her from the pack. In his book of the expedition, *South*, Shackleton wrote: 'I . . . sent all hands on to the floe with ice-chisels, prickers, saws and picks. All that day and most of the next we worked strenuously to get the ship into the lead ahead of us. After terrific labour . . . about 400 yards of heavy ice still separated *Endurance* from the water, and reluctantly I was compelled to admit that further effort was useless.'

1

2

3

2 The crew of *Endurance* playing a football
  match on the ice floe, 16 February 1915. Dr
  Macklin was, as Orde-Lees wrote in his
  diary that day, the 'much needed and
  capable referee'.
3 The night watch was taken in turns, but
  frequently others not on duty would join the
  watchman at his warm stove and, as Hurley
  put it, 'discourse in subdued whispers'.

Clark returning from winter exercise (usually known as 'The Night Watchman Returns'). Shackleton realised that the great enemy of the men during the winter months was boredom and he encouraged them to take exercise. Orde-Lees, for example, rode his bicycle on the ice, whilst others tried to learn to ski.

1   2   3

1 Captain Frank Worsley was a brilliant navigator. Shackleton recognised this skill, which was put to the test both en route to Elephant Island and then on the open boat journey to South Georgia, where a navigational error would have meant the difference between life and death. Using a sextant under those conditions required coordination and delicacy of no mean order. But it also required instinct. Shackleton understood and respected that. Worsley captained Shackleton's last expedition ship, *Quest*, in 1921–2.

2 Tom Crean was an Irishman with an ability to endure inconceivably unpleasant conditions with good humour. He had excelled himself on Scott's 1911 expedition when he and another naval rating had rescued Lieutenant Teddy Evans and dragged him fifty miles to safety on a sledge. Crean trusted Shackleton's instincts completely and never questioned his leadership. He was rewarded for this loyalty by being selected to sail with the *James Caird* and later to cross South Georgia with Shackleton and Worsley.

3 Frank Wild was Shackleton's second in command. He was able to get on with all the men, whatever their station, without losing his authority. On the *Endurance* expedition he was the man Shackleton entrusted with the safety of the men marooned on Elephant Island while he sailed for help. It was the right choice. The men respected and trusted him. According to Macklin he was '. . . a magnificent leader here, scrupulously fair in everything, and popular and respected by everyone.'

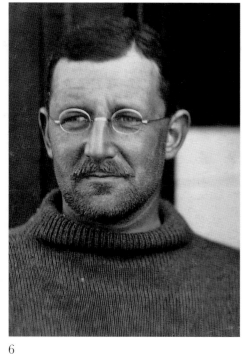

4

5

6

4 George Marston had been on *Nimrod* as the expedition artist. He had a penchant for dressing up in women's clothes whenever an entertainment was proposed, lipstick, rouge et al. As an artist he was able to capture the drama and terror of a moment in a way that a photographer could not. He worked with Hurley to produce some composite images using photographs and paint.

5 Percy Blackborrow, here pictured with Mrs Chippy, the cat belonging to the ship's carpenter, McNeish, had stowed away in Buenos Aires, aided by two other crew members who thought *Endurance* was short-staffed. Shackleton was apoplectic with rage when Blackborrow was discovered but was forced to admit that they were a man short and could make good use of him. At nineteen he became the youngest member of the crew and proved to be an able seaman.

6 Dr Alexander Macklin was the expedition's chief surgeon. His interest in polar matters dated back to his student days and as soon as he saw Shackleton's advertisement he applied to join *Endurance*. When Shackleton asked him in the interview what was wrong with his eyes (Macklin wore spectacles) he replied, 'Nothing,' and then added, 'many a wise face would look foolish without specs.' Shackleton laughed and offered him a place.

8

9

10

7 'The Boss', the name conferred on Shackleton during the *Nimrod* expedition by Frank Wild, was universally admired and trusted. 'To serve such a leader,' Orde-Lees wrote, 'is one of the greatest pleasures of the whole trip . . . he knows one's limitations better than one does oneself and he invariably allows for them . . . he trusts one implicitly and he always appears to be pleased with what one has done.'

8 As the expedition's photographer, Frank Hurley was not there just to record events; he was also an artist and he set up and created some of the most evocative images ever to come out of Antarctica. Greenstreet described him as 'a warrior with his camera', who 'would go anywhere or do anything to get a picture'.

9 Thomas Hans Orde-Lees was also an Anglo-Irishman. A born outsider, he came into conflict with most of the crew for one reason or another. He kept a diary that revealed shrewd observations of his fellow men as well as wistful thoughts. In January 1915 he wrote: 'I do wish sometimes, that I could just pop home for an hour or two as easily in the flesh as in the spirit. No doubt the explorers of 2015, if there is anything left to explore, will not only carry their pocket wireless telephones fitted with wireless telescopes but will also receive their nourishment and warmth by wireless . . .'

10 James Mann Wordie was a geologist from Cambridge who joined the expedition as a member of the scientific team. After returning from *Endurance* and war service he became a Fellow of St John's College, Cambridge and eventually was Master of the College. The papers he published in 1921 on oceanography, geology and the polar ice pack represent the main scientific results of the expedition.

1 John Vincent making a net. He was a
trawler hand and as such well practised at
the task, but he was not an especially liked
member of the mess-deck. This is a
particularly good example of the Paget-
colour plate technique that Frank Hurley
experimented with during the expedition.
Paget-colour plates pre-date colour film;
thirty-two plates exist from *Endurance*.

2 This photograph of *Endurance* was taken at
sunrise in April 1915. Hurley had helped
with the construction of 'rickers' in the
riggings, which were put in place to help the
ship receive Morse Code signals. This
ingenious idea was typical of Hurley's
pragmatic approach, but the rickers had to
be abandoned as they soon became covered
with thick rime, rendering them useless.

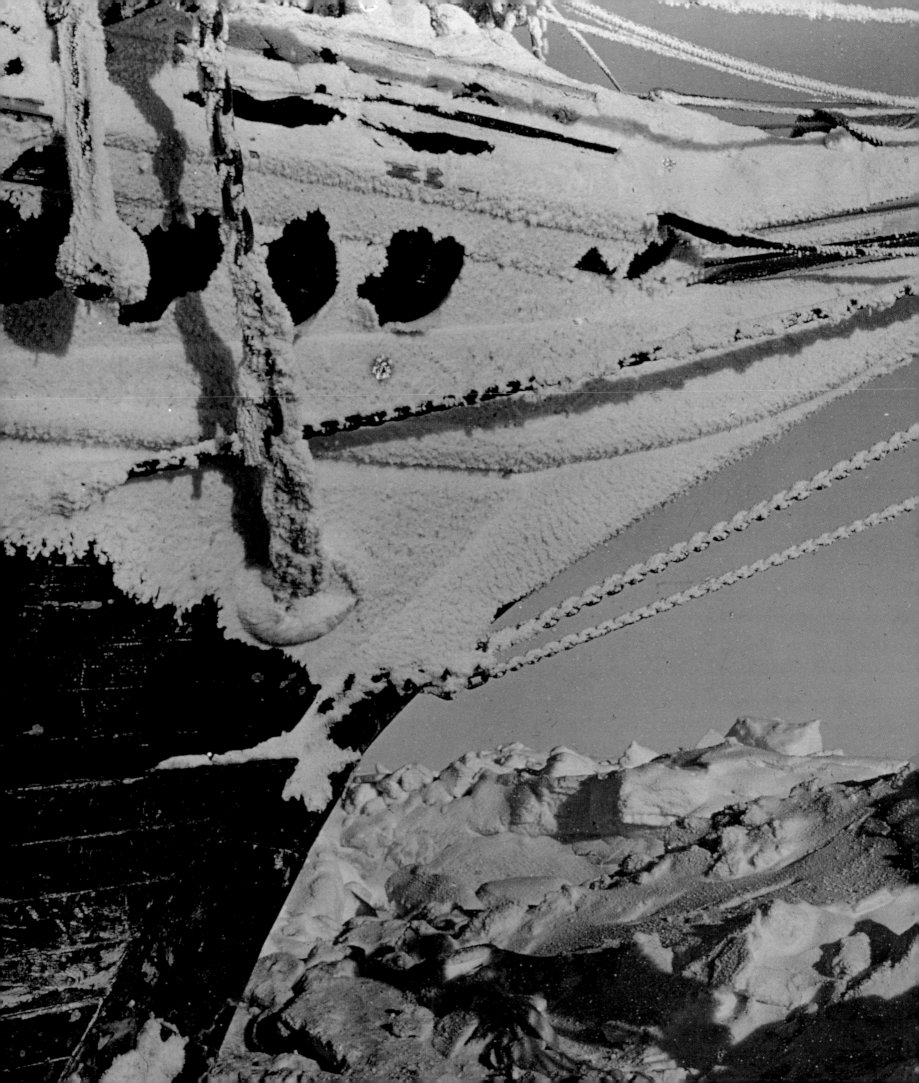

Previous page: Hurley was principally responsible for making a cinematographic film of the expedition, although his still photographs were to be his most important legacy. His images of *Endurance* in her death throes count among the most extraordinary scenes captured on film.

1 Hurley captures the sense of desolation of the icepack.

2 Reginald James hoisting the red ensign and the Australian flag. James was a physicist from Cambridge. Prior to sailing with *Endurance* he had led a sheltered life, being brought up by two maiden aunts. In the tough circumstances to which he was subjected on the expedition, he proved himself to be adaptable, although he was mocked by everyone for being clumsy. Greenstreet noted in his diary that when James was witnessed dropping test tubes he was heard to let fire a string of expletives, which, it was concluded, he had most certainly not learned from his aunts.

2

These two photographs were taken close to
the Antarctic midwinter. The sun
disappeared for some 120 days, although
there was often a little light from the Aurora
Australis. Beautiful though the images are,
the Antarctic winter on *Endurance* was long
and difficult. The men were caught in a
frozen trap with little to do other than to
attend to the daily routine: 'No outside
work,' McNeish recorded in his diary, 'only
arguments about the war . . .'

1 Hussey holding Samson. The photograph is sometimes captioned 'The smallest man with the biggest dog'. Hussey was of a cheerful disposition. His selection had been typically haphazard; he had seen Shackleton's advertisement in an old newspaper he was reading on an archaeological dig in the Sudan. He wrote to Shackleton and received the reply that he should make contact. Shackleton had apparently been amused to receive a request to go to the Antarctic from the heart of Africa.

2 Alexander Macklin was responsible for one of the six teams of dogs on *Endurance*. Compared with the earlier expeditions, the dogs were treated well and were given exercise. Their masters were even attempting to learn the art of dog-driving. Rivalry between the teams developed and an Antarctic Derby was held in midwinter. Wild's team won with an average speed over a 700-yard course of ten and a half miles per hour.

3 Initially the dogs were kept on the upper deck. They made entertaining companions and gave the men something to occupy their time and energy. Later they were moved onto the ice, where 'dogloos', like small igloos, were constructed for them.

Shackleton's cabin on *Endurance*. It had originally been Worsley's. McNeish, the carpenter, installed the bogie and insulated the cabin in March 1915 in preparation for the long Antarctic winter. Shackleton's books included volumes on polar exploration and he encouraged his men to borrow them. He was concerned with the men's learning and would question them when they returned the books to him.

1

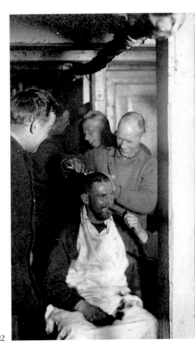

2

1 In March 1915 Shackleton ordered the 'tween-decks to be fitted out as a living and dining room for the officers and scientists. The new quarters immediately became known as 'The Ritz' and very soon a 'winter routine' was established, involving the necessary and unpopular twice-weekly task of scrubbing the floor. Everyone had to undertake this work, whatever their station. Here James Wordie, Alfred Cheetham and Alexander Macklin are taking their turn.

2 During the winter the men decided to shave off all their hair. Hurley called it 'a form of midwinter madness', and he wrote in his diary: 'It caused much amusement, and luxuriant curls, bald pates and parted crowns soon became akin. We are likely to be cool-headed in the future if not neuralgic. We resemble a cargo of convicts . . .'

3 A midwinter morning in 'The Ritz'. On the left, behind McNeish, is Blackborrow carrying a large block of ice to the galley.

4 Midwinter's Day, 22 June 1915. It was a tradition amongst Antarctic explorers to celebrate midwinter and to herald the return of the sun, harbinger of better days to come. McNeish noted in his diary that their celebratory meal included 'roast pork, stewed apples and preserved peas with plum pudding'.

3

4

After dinner there was an entertainment
performed by the men for Shackleton. The
majority of them dressed up and sang songs
or recited verses. James McIlroy appeared
as the perfumed grisette – his presentation
was not considered acceptable for polite
British society.

'One feels our helplessness as the long winter night closes upon us. By this time, if fortune had smiled upon the Expedition, we would have been comfortably and securely established in a shore base . . . Where will we make a landing now? . . . Time alone will tell.'

From Shackleton's diary, when the sun disappeared for the winter, 1 May 1915

1

1 In the middle of July 1915 McNeish noted
   in his diary that there was a 'slight shock'.
   It was the ice moving. Shackleton, although
   outwardly optimistic, confided in Worsley
   that he thought the ship was near her end.
   Worsley later wrote: 'The wind howled in
   the rigging and I couldn't help thinking it
   was making just the sort of sound you
   would expect a human being to utter if they
   were in fear of being murdered . . . Still I
   couldn't believe *Endurance* would have to go
   . . . "The ship can't live like this, Skipper,"
   . . . Shackleton . . . said at length, pausing in
   his restless march up and down the tiny
   cabin. "You had better make up your mind
   that it is only a matter of time . . . What the
   ice gets, the ice keeps."

2 In *South* Shackleton described *Endurance*'s
   final days: 'The pack was working, and the
   roar of pressure ever and anon was heard.
   We waited for the next move of the gigantic
   forces arrayed against us, and on Sunday,
   October 24th, the beginning of the end for
   Endurance came. The position was lat. 69, 11'
   S., long. 51 5' W. . . . The ship groaned and
   quivered as her starboard quarter was
   forced against the floe twisting the stern-
   post and starting the heads and ends of
   planking.'

2

'For sudden the worst turns the best to the brave.'

Shackleton's favourite quotation from 'Prospice' by Robert Browning

1, 2 As *Endurance* was slowly crushed by the ice, Shackleton was overcome by emotion: 'It is hard to write what I feel. To a sailor his ship is more than a floating home, and in *Endurance* I had centred ambitions, hopes and desires. And now she is slowly giving up her sentient life at the very outset of her career.'

3 Wild, Shackleton and Hurley made the last 'official' visit to the wreck on 8 November 1915. Two weeks later *Endurance* finally sank. On 21 November Shackleton wrote in his diary: 'At 5 pm she went down by the head: the stern the cause of all the trouble was the last to go under water. I cannot write about it.'

'Put footstep of courage into stirrup of patience.'

From Shackleton's diary, while on the ice after abandoning *Endurance*, 19 November 1915

1, 2 'Ocean Camp', Shackleton's first camp on the floe after abandoning *Endurance*. Amongst the many problems Shackleton encountered was a lack of adequate equipment. There were only eighteen reindeer sleeping bags for twenty-eight men. They were shared by rota, the remaining ten men made do with blanket bags.

3 Shackleton was faced with the task of keeping up the morale of his men. One of the ways he did this was to encourage as much 'normal' activity as possible. Worsley had an observation platform, Hussey his meteorological instruments. In addition, Shackleton increased the men's food rations so that they should not feel hungry. Macklin wrote in his diary on 8 December: 'an anxious time . . . but everybody is cheerful . . . We are getting a pretty good allowance of food, and we have adapted ourselves pretty well to this tent life . . . If we come through alive and safe it will be a great experience to look back on.'

2

3

'Called by Hurley 4.30 am to see a crack
running through the camp traced it to
pressure crack just opening . . . 8 am shifted
camp away from crack. Hope now secure:
Everywhere signs of ice breaking up . . . Got
lat. 66°59'30". 52.46' W. slow going but I
think our good time is coming.'

From Shackleton's diary, 30 December 1915

'Sent Crean Lees Macklin with 2 dog teams to Ocean Camp . . . they returned . . . with stores & literature . . . Trust this waiting will soon be over. It has now been more than a year.'

From Shackleton's diary when at Patience Camp, 30 January 1916

'We have done well under Providence up to now. Oh for a touch of dry land under our feet.'

From Shackleton's diary, 9 February 1916

1 Shackleton and Hurley at Patience Camp. Hurley was inventive and practically very resourceful, designing a stove which, according to James, 'acted like a blast furnace'. Here he is skinning a penguin.

2 Potash and Perlmutter were the names given to Orde-Lees and Green. Their 'galley on ice' with their cooking supplies and kitchen stores was black with grime from the blubber stove but a cheerful corner of the camp. There was a steady supply of seal and penguin, which provided meat for the men, their forty-nine dogs and Mrs Chippy (the cat).

3 In certain practical ways Shackleton was way ahead of his time. The tents for the *Endurance* expedition, designed by himself and Marston, were dome-shaped for better wind resistance and much easier to pitch than previous designs.

2

3

1 The men's one hope for escape from the ice were the lifeboats, now named the *James Caird*, *Dudley Docker* and *Stancomb-Wills*, after three of the principle backers of the expedition. The boats had to be dragged across the ice with the rest of the sledges and equipment. The *James Caird* weighed over a ton and the hummocky ice made moving her a stupendous task.

2 The *Dudley Docker* arriving on Elephant Island, 15 April 1916. After six days at sea and three nights without sleep, the men were exhausted, seasick, thirsty and frostbitten, but they had succeeded in finding Elephant Island, which was to be their temporary home for four months.

3 Handling the *James Caird* on Providence Beach. Elephant Island was inhospitable by any standards, but, despite the lack of vegetation, it provided plenty of fresh food in the form of penguin and seal and there was unlimited fresh water from the glacier. Above all, it was *terra firma*.

1, 2 Launching the *James Caird*, 24 April 1916, for the greatest open boat journey in history. 'The perils of the proposed journey were extreme,' Shackleton wrote in his book *South*, 'and the risk was justified solely by our urgent need of assistance. The ocean south of Cape Horn in the middle of May is known to be the most tempestuous area of water in the world and the gales are almost unceasing. We had to face these conditions in a small and weather-beaten boat, already strained by the work of the previous months.'

3 The *James Caird* was launched with Worsley, Crean, Shackleton, McNeish, Vincent and McCarthy as the crew. It was a strong team, so Shackleton believed, but nevertheless he was in no doubt that sailing in the tumultuous southern oceans their voyage 'would be a big adventure'.

April 23rd 1916 Elephant Island

Dear Sir,
In the event of my not surviving the boat journey to
South Georgia you will do your best for the rescue of the
party. You are in full command from the time the boat
leaves this island, and all hands are under your orders. On
your return to England you are to communicate with the
Committee. I wish you, Lees and Hurley to write the
book. You watch my interests. In another letter you will

find the terms as agreed for lecturing you to do England Great Britain & Continent. Hurley the USA. I have every confidence in you and always have had. May God prosper your work and your life. You can convey my love to my people and say I tried my best.

Yours sincerely,

Ernest. H. Shackleton.

Shackleton's letter to Frank Wild before setting out on the open boat journey

Previous page: The twenty-two men remaining on Elephant Island now had to put all their trust in Shackleton's ability to survive even the most extreme circumstances. Hurley wrote in his diary on the day of the *James Caird*'s departure: 'Great confidence is reposed in the crew: six proven veterans, seasoned by the salt & experience of the Sea . . . The *Caird* is an excellent sailer, & guided by Providence, should make Sth. Georgia in 14 days . . . How we shall count the days.'

1 The 'hut' on Elephant Island was made out of the two remaining lifeboats and sheltered twenty-two men for four months. The floor space measured nineteen feet by ten feet, and there was no room to stand upright. Its foundations were an old penguin rookery, so the smell was unpleasant before they even started, but at least it sheltered them from the weather. Hurley described the interior as 'a catacomb like scene of objects resembling mummies. These objects are us in reindeer sleeping bags mingling our snores with the roar of the blizzard.'

2 The men left behind on Elephant Island – 'the most motley and unkempt assemblage that ever was projected on a plate', as Hurley noted in his diary on 10 May 1916, two weeks after the *James Caird* had sailed. The photograph is sometimes captioned 'The Marooned Party'.

' . . . pleasant calm day, though dull. During the morning go walking with Wild. We visited a neighbouring cavern in the glacier which was adorned with a magnificence of icicles.'

From Hurley's diary, 5 July 1916

1 Geer Buttress and Hooke Glacier, South
Georgia. On the back of this photograph
Worsley had written, 'Some of the
mountains we marched across'.
Shackleton, Crean and Worsley walked
from King Haakon Bay on the west of the
island to Stromness in thirty-six hours,
arriving on the afternoon of 19 May 1916.

2 Bull elephant seals, after which Elephant
Island was named. When Shackleton and
his men arrived there, there were no
elephant seals on the island, as they had
been hunted to extinction.

3 On 30 August 1916, Shackleton returned
to fetch the twenty-two men left behind on
Elephant Island. Describing the rescue in
South, he wrote: 'I saw a little figure on a
surf-beaten rock and recognised Wild. As I
came nearer I called out, "Are you all
well?" and he answered, "We are all well,
Boss," and then I heard three cheers . . .
Wild had kept hope alive in their hearts.'
Shackleton did not even step onto
Elephant Island. The party was rescued
with all possible speed and within an hour
they were steaming north on *Yelcho*.

3

'I cannot settle down to anything whilst my mind is on those ten men of mine in the Ross Sea.'

From Shackleton's letter to Janet Stancomb-Wills, written in Buenos Aires on the way to the Ross Sea, 4 October 1916

2

1 Shackleton, Wild and others in Punta
   Arenas on 3 September 1916. Now that the
   Elephant Island men had been rescued,
   Shackleton's attentions turned towards the
   Ross Sea party.

2 The rescued party photographed in front of
   the Royal Hotel, Punta Arenas, where,
   according to Shackleton in his book *South*,
   they were given a welcome they would
   never forget: 'The whole populace appeared
   to be in the streets. It was a great reception,
   and after the long, anxious months of strain
   we were in a mood to enjoy it.'

6

QUEST: THE SHACKLETON-ROWETT EXPEDITION 1921-2

Opposite: This studio photograph was signed by Shackleton and given to John Quiller Rowett just before his departure on Quest in 1921. Right: Cablegram sent by Shackleton to Macklin, to whom he had passed responsibility for stocking Quest and getting all the equipment ready.

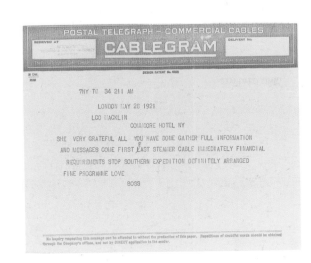

After *Endurance*, Shackleton once more became the fluid, drifting personality of his shoregoing self, to which there was now added a melancholy suggestion of decay. He was drinking too much. He wanted to fight, but was unable to join up. The Army wanted men, but not Shackleton, it seemed. After a desultory stint of propaganda service in South America, and an abortive, murky undercover operation in the Arctic, he was recalled to London, to become a soldier at last. Gazetted a temporary Major, he was sent to Northern Russia, arriving a fortnight before the Armistice on 11 November 1918. He became involved in the Allied war of intervention against the Bolsheviks, supposedly as an expert in winter transport. By March 1919, he was demobilised and thrown on his own devices once more.

He was like a relic from another world. All his fortune-hunting had failed. Money he had none. He tried lecturing on the *Endurance* expedition. Twice daily he gave a live commentary on Hurley's silent film on the subject. Finally, the book of the expedition, dictated to a secretary, like *The Heart of the Antarctic*, was published as *South* at the end of 1919. None of this gave him money or satisfaction. Once more he was reduced to living on his wits. At least, he seemed to have preserved his gift for making contact with moneyed men. One of them was an old school friend, John Quiller Rowett.

Rowett willingly succumbed to Shackleton's spell and helped conjure up another expedition, originally intended for the Canadian Arctic, and when that failed, to turn south again. His ship this time was a hastily acquired Norwegian sealer called *Foca I*, which Shackleton renamed *Quest*. Only 125 tons burden, she was in poor condition. On 17 September 1921, *Quest* sailed from St Katharine's Dock, under Tower Bridge.

On board were Shackleton's particular friends from *Endurance*: Worsley, Macklin, McIlroy and Wild. They had come from the ends of the earth. The

purpose of the voyage was supposedly to circumnavigate Antarctica, looking for lost sub-polar islands. As a publicity stunt, an eighteen-year-old Boy Scout called James Marr was taken along. On the surface this seemed like one more hopeful enterprise of Shackleton's. Underneath, however, there was something indefinably different. It was like a reunion rather than an expedition. Nor was it quite the old Shackleton who was on board. His familiar, impressive seagoing self was mostly absent. Those who had not known him before could only glimpse at what he had once been like. He was altogether calmer now, quieter and unnaturally relaxed. Mostly, he seemed only to want to relive old times with his old companions. Even to them, however, he was not the man they once had known.

Macklin was the man most troubled by all this. As Shackleton's doctor, he saw worrying changes. Shackleton was listless, uncharacteristically leaving others to organise and make decisions. He was drinking heavily. And at Buenos Aires, when the ship called there, he had had what appeared to be another heart attack. Moreover, he still refused to let any doctor, even Macklin, examine him.

Shackleton was harping on the past and his unrelenting scorn of Scott welled up. He was brooding on the promise extracted from him not to go to McMurdo Sound on *Nimrod* in 1908. Heading now for

A cairn surmounted with a cross was erected by Shackleton's comrades on the slopes of Duse Fell in South Georgia to commemorate his death.

South Georgia, he wanted to revisit the scene of the one ambition that he had fulfilled: the saving of his men and the accomplishment of a great open boat journey. After South Georgia, however, he had no plans. When all was said and done, what he was trying to make was a voyage back in time.

On 4 January 1922, *Quest* arrived at South Georgia. She anchored off Grytviken, the whaling station that Shackleton had entered with such hope on the start of his journey in 1914. It was another world now. The whalers he had known, and whom he went ashore to meet, had changed too. It was not a happy revival of things past: reunions rarely are. This one was made even less happy by the fact that Shackleton was still dwelling on the fuss made over Scott's spectacular death, while his own accomplishments were dimmed. He talked about it when he returned on board for the night.

In the early hours of the morning of 5 January 1922, Macklin was called to Shackleton's cabin, and found him having another heart attack. In a short time he was dead.

Under Wild's command, *Quest* carried on for a spell, sailing to Elephant Island for a bitter-sweet return. But now it was a hollow enterprise. Soon the expedition was brought to a premature end and the members went their different ways.

Shackleton's body started its journey back home for burial. Emily, however, decided that his final resting place could not be in the British Isles, where he had never really felt at ease. In the end, although by now all but abandoned as a wife, it was she who most clearly saw the human being behind the outer shell. So from Montevideo, Shackleton was brought back to South Georgia and buried among the whalers, an outcast among the outcasts to whom he truly belonged. His monument was a simple cross on a height overlooking the waters.

1

1, 2 Shackleton and *Quest* at St Katharine's Dock, London. The Shackleton-Rowett expedition had as its aim the circumnavigation of the Antarctic continent. *Quest* was a wooden sealer, of 125 tons. Purchased by Shackleton on a visit to Norway, she would have been better suited to Arctic travel than to a long trip across the Atlantic.

2

3 Shackleton's cabin aboard *Quest*. As was customary, Shackleton fitted out his cabin with reading matter and a very few luxuries. For the first time, however, he had electric light in his living quarters.

4 Selecting a Boy Scout to accompany the expedition was a publicity stunt organised by the *Daily Mail*. The boy chosen, James Marr (wearing a kilt, second from the right) was later to become an explorer in his own right and was never comfortable with the role wished upon him on *Quest*. He was supposed to ghostwrite the book of the expedition for Shackleton.

I

1 Shackleton and Rowett had been friends at Dulwich College and had corresponded intermittently over the years. Rowett was a very wealthy man, having made his fortune in rum. He agreed to fund Shackleton's expedition in the same spirit of charitable generosity as had Sir James Caird the *Endurance* in 1914.

2 Shackleton with Charles Green. Green had been the cook on *Endurance* and had spent all his time on the ice floes and indeed on Elephant Island looking after the needs of the men. On *Quest* Shackleton took with him several members of the *Endurance* expedition, partly, perhaps, because he wanted the 'old guard' around him as he made what he probably knew was his final voyage.

3 London bids farewell to Shackleton. Emily was not at St Katharine's Dock to see *Quest* sail, but Rosalind Chetwynd had made an inspection of the ship before she left, and had made a gift for Shackleton of three white polo-neck sweaters.

2

The crowds on St. Katharine's Wharf waving good-bye.

3

1.

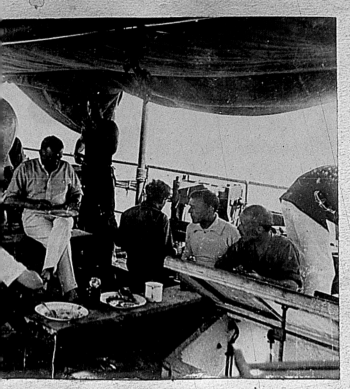

g lunch on deck.

Green, (the cook).

Command

Lunch on deck.

lunch on deck.

for lunch on deck.

'. . . It is only by constant thought and care that the leader can lead. There is a delightful sense of freedom from responsibility in all others, and it should be so. These are just random thoughts: but borne in on one as it all being so different for [sic] the other strain of preparation: it is a blessing that this time I have not the financial worry or strain to add to the care of the active Expedition.'

From Shackleton's diary, 29 November 1921

1 These photographs capture the relaxed mood of the voyage of *Quest* in warm climes on its outward journey. Shackleton is sitting among the men enjoying lunch on deck. Wild observed that the Boss was content to enjoy the camaraderie of his men and wrote that he 'seemed to be enjoying the quiet, the freedom and the mental peace of our small self-contained world'.

2 Shackleton and Wild sailing southwards on *Quest*, reminiscing about the past. The other members of the expedition recorded in their diaries and letters how Shackleton liked to talk about the old days. They also observed that he only occasionally showed flashes of his former spirit. Macklin found him listless and enigmatic, and as a doctor he was also concerned about the Boss's health.

2

1 On the way to South Georgia, heeling to
  port, *Quest* 'lumbered heavily in the trade
  winds'. She was not well suited to a long
  voyage across the Atlantic and at every port
  they found she needed repairs.

2 Commander Wild in the crow's-nest.
  Wild was, as ever, Shackleton's closest
  lieutenant. He had been with Shackleton on
  all four of his expeditions and had even
  joined him, at Shackleton's request, on the
  Northern Russia campaign.

2

1 Leonard Hussey taking the water
   temperature. Hussey, who for so many
   months had kept the men on *Endurance*
   entertained with his banjo and limited
   repertoire of songs, was another to whom
   Shackleton felt a sense of loyalty. He
   accepted Shackleton's invitation
   immediately he received the cable and
   brought his banjo – the one that had made
   it to Elephant Island – with him.
2 Shackleton washing a dog on board *Quest*.

3

3 Of Worsley, here pictured using a sextant, Shackleton had written in *South*, 'I had a very high opinion of his accuracy and quickness as a navigator – an opinion that was only enhanced during our [open boat] journey.' It was clear that Worsley would be asked to captain *Quest*.

4 Shackleton's letter to John Quiller Rowett, written on 18 December 1921 from Rio de Janeiro. It contains his most popular rallying cry, 'Never for me the lowered banner, Never the lost endeavour', from the poem 'Cor Cordium' by the Celtic Twilight poet Fiona Macleod.

QUEST. R.Y.S.

2

will have nothing to do
with anything wrong with
the ship. The ship is right
Give Ellie my love and
tell her that—
"Never for me the lowered banner"
"Never the lost endeavour"
Your friend
Ernest

4

'At last after 16 days of turmoil and anxiety: on a peaceful sunshiny day we came to an anchor in Grytviken. How familiar the coast seemed as we passed down: we saw with full interest the places we struggled over after the boat journey.'

From Shackleton's diary, 4 January 1922

Previous page: 'Where the "Boss" died, Duse Fell.' Macklin wrote this simple but poignant caption below this image of Grytviken harbour taken from his album. Shackleton succumbed to a massive heart attack in the early hours of 5 January 1922. He was forty-seven years old. Before he left England he had told an admirer that 'he did not mean to die in Europe'.

1 Shackleton's body was taken from Grytviken to Montevideo with the intention of bringing it back to Britain but when Emily learned of her husband's death she immediately insisted that he would rather be buried on South Georgia, his spiritual home. Here in Montevideo, his coffin is draped in his own flag. Thousands of people thronged the streets to pay their last respects to the great man.

2 Sir Ernest Shackleton's coffin being loaded onto a gun carriage in preparation for a procession through the streets of Montevideo.

1 Shackleton's coffin being carried from the Whaler's Church, South Georgia on 5 March 1922. None of his closest friends were able to attend the funeral, as *Quest* was still heading south under Wild's command.

2, 3 The committal: Shackleton was buried alongside the whalers, outcasts from society amongst whom he had felt strangely at home. It was the whalers who recognised better than any other what he had achieved, particularly on the open boat journey in 1916, for their knowledge of the southern oceans told them he should not have survived.

1, 2 In May 1922, Wild, now in charge of *Quest*, brought the expedition back to South Georgia to visit Shackleton's grave and to erect a cairn in his memory. Leonard Hussey expressed the sentiments of all his companions when he wrote of their leader, in a letter to H.R. Mill, 'For us he had faults but no vices . . . He had a way of compelling loyalty. We would have gone anywhere without question just on his order . . . Now that he has gone, there is a gap in our lives that can never be filled.'

3 A.B. McLeod at Shackleton's memorial. The cairn was erected on a promontory overlooking Grytviken harbour, vulnerable to the wind, snow, ice and sea – the elemental forces that had inspired Shackleton's life. It was here that Emily knew her husband's heart lay, not in the gentle landscape of England.

3

QUEST. R.Y.S.

The plate on the cairn was engraved like this

SIR ERNEST SHACKLETON
EXPLORER.
DIED HERE JAN 5th 1922
ERECTED
BY HIS COMRADES.

The Cairn.

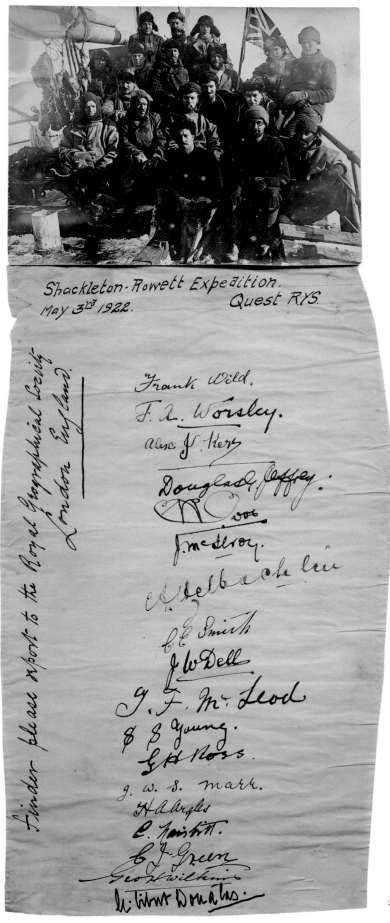

1 A sketch of the memorial cairn with its inscription dedicated to the memory of Ernest Shackleton.
2 Shackleton-Rowett Expedition photograph, left beneath Shackleton's grave on 3 May 1922. Shackleton was a great leader, who valued the lives of those under his command more highly than his own personal ambition. It was this outstanding quality that so endeared him to the men whose loyalty he deserved and cherished.

2

Epilogue

With Shackleton there came to an end the so-called heroic age of Antarctic exploration. This was the predominantly British fight during the first decades of the twentieth century to be first at the South Pole. Its hallmark was sheer human struggle before the final advent of mechanical transport.

The heroic aspect of the process had its roots in the Romantic movement, which equated heroism more with suffering than achievement. Of that, Shackleton was the pre-eminent exponent. He saw in the Antarctic a stage on which to project himself as hero. He was distinguished by possessing all the heroic qualities. Above all, he was a survivor. He cared about his men.

His misfortune was that of being unsuited to his chosen task. He lacked the winning touch. His fate was to be the man who showed the way. He pioneered the road to the South Pole to within the last hundred miles. And in the end the man who finished the job was someone with no heroic pretensions at all. Roald Amundsen, the Norwegian who was first at the South Pole merely wanted to win the race. He turned it into an intellectual achievement, thereby defacing the picture of glory demanded by the public.

That left Shackleton as the melancholy baffled hero. He was a transitional figure; the last of the old explorers, and the first of the modern adventurers. His attempt to cross Antarctica, in the light of history, seems the earliest of the artificial goals contrived by them to extract a field of endeavour from the shrinking spaces of the unknown. It was the prelude to the final first crossing of the continent four decades later, led by Sir Vivian Fuchs. He, however, used motor transport. It was three-quarters of a century before the first attainment of the feat by the classical method of dogs and sledges, under the American Will Steger in 1989–90, but his supplies were dropped by air along the way. And behind them always loomed Shackleton the precursor.

For long, Shackleton languished in the shades, half forgotten. Scott held the limelight, because of the public taste for the glorious failure and the elegiac hero. Finally, Shackleton came into his own, at least in the Anglo-Saxon world, as the ultimate survivor. After two world wars, and the opening of the nuclear age, survival was finally honoured above self-sacrifice.

Even in his best moments in the public eye, however, Shackleton had always seemed somehow out of his element. He was the everlasting outsider; the misfit with no place in civilised society.

In many ways, he was the Homeric hero: a very human figure whose virtues were balanced by his faults.

Previous page: The crew of
Quest *with Shackleton in the*
centre. During his last
expedition he was surrounded
by loyal friends and memories
of happier times.

In retrospect, the *Quest* expedition appears as a deliberately chosen end, away from the society in which Shackleton was adulated for a season, but never really accepted. Shackleton's end was like that of Ulysses, as portrayed by Dante in the *Inferno*:

> né dolcezza di figlio, né la pieta
> del vecchio padre, né 'l debito amore
> lo qual dovea Penelopè far lieta
>
> vincer potero dentro a me l'ardore
> ch'i' ebbi a divenir del mondo esperto
> e de li vizi umani e del valore;
>
> ma misi me per l'alto mare aperto
> sol con un legno e con quella compagna
> picciola da la qual non fui diserto . . .
>
> 'O frati', dissi, 'che per cento milia
> perigli siete giunti . . .
>
> a questa tanto picciola vigilia
> de' nostri sensi ch'è del rimanente
> non vogliate negar l'esperïenza,
> di retro al sol, del mondo sanza gente.

(canto xxvi 94–117)

No tenderness for my son, nor piety
To my old father, nor the wedded love
That should have comforted Penelope

Could conquer in me the restless itch to rove
And rummage through the world exploring it,
All human worth and wickedness to prove.

So on the deep and open sea I set
Forth, with a single ship and that small band
Of comrades that had never left me yet . . .

'Brothers,' said I, 'that have come valiantly
Through hundred thousand jeopardies undergone
. . . you will not now deny

To this last little vigil left to run
Of feeling life, the new experience
Of the uninhabited world behind the sun.'

(Translated by Dorothy L. Sayers)

Index

Picture Credits

t = top; b = bottom; l = left; r = right; c = centre; cl = centre left; cr = centre right; fl = far left; fr = far right

© CHRISTIE'S IMAGES LTD, LONDON, 2002
2, 4 (cl, cr), 5 (fl, cl, cr, fr), 13, 15, 17 (l, r), 23, 25, 34–5, 49 (b), 57 (t), 80, 83, 104, 106 (tl), 107, 130 (t, b), 131, 144 (b), 149, 152, 160, 163, 164, 167, 170, 179, 185, 188, 190, 192, 194 (tl, b), 195, 196–7, 198, 199, 202, 212, 229, 237 (b), 252, 253, 254 (b), 257, 259 (t), 263, 266 (b), 267 (t, b), 276, 279

© CLAYESMORE SCHOOL, 2002
154

© DULWICH COLLEGE ARCHIVE, LONDON, 2002
18 (t, b), 26, 261 (b)

EDWARD BINNIE COLLECTION © THOMAS BINNIE JNR, 2002
272 (t), 273

© ILLUSTRATED LONDON NEWS, 2002
85, 150, 156

© MITCHELL LIBRARY, STATE LIBRARY OF NEW SOUTH WALES, 2002
214, 215, 216–17, 218, 219, 220, 221, 257, 260, 263, 264, 265, 266 (t), 268–9, 274 (t, b), 275

© NATIONAL PORTRAIT GALLERY, LONDON , 2002
165 (tl)

© PRIVATE COLLECTION, 2002
1, 12, 16, 19, 21, 84, 109, 148, 165, 254 (t), 261 (b), 262

© ROYAL GEOGRAPHICAL SOCIETY, LONDON, 2002
22, 27, 28, 29, 30, 33, 37, 40, 41 (t), 42 (t, b), 43, 44, 45, 46 (t, b), 47, 48, 49 (t), 50, 51 (t, b), 52–3 (c), 54 (b), 56 (t), 57 (b), 61, 62 (t, b), 63, 64, 65, 66, 67, 68, 72 (b), 74–5, 74 (b), 76 (t, b), 78, 81, 90, 92, 93, 94,

97 (t, b), 100, 103, 104, 106 (r), 108, 109 (r), 110 (l, r), 111, 112, 113, 114 (l, br), 115 (t, b), 116–17, 119, 120, 121 (t), 122 (t, b), 123, 124 (t, bl, br), 125, 126, 127 (b), 128 (b), 129 (tl, b), 133, 134, 135, 136 (tl), 146 (t), 166, 169, 172, 173, 174, 177, 182, 200, 203, 204–5, 206 (t, b), 207, 209, 210 (r, c), 222, 223 (b), 224, 226 (t), 227 (t, b), 230, 231, 232 (l, r), 233, 234, 235 (t, b), 236, 237 (t), 238 (t, b), 239, 240 (t, b), 241, 242–3, 244, 245, 246–7, 248, 249 (b), 250, 277, 283

© SCOTT POLAR RESEARCH INSTITUTE, CAMBRIDGE, 2002
4 (fl, fr), 7, 9, 14, 32, 36, 38, 39, 41 (b), 52 (l), 53 (r), 54 (t), 55 (t, b), 56 (b), 58–9, 60, 69, 70–1, 72–3 (t), 79, 82, 87, 88, 89, 95, 96, 98, 99, 102, 105 (t, b), 118, 121 (b), 127 (t), 128 (t), 129 (cr), 132, 136 (b), 138, 139, 140, 141, 142, 143, 144 (t), 145, 146 (b), 147, 159, 161, 162 (tr, bl), 168, 210 (l), 211 (l, c, r), 213 (l, c, r), 223 (t), 226 (b), 228, 249 (t), 251, 254 (b), 255, 258 (t, b), 259 (b), 261 (t), 270, 271, 272 (b)

Every effort has been made to trace the source of these pictures. Should there be any unintentional omissions the publisher will be happy to include them in a future edition.

Acknowledgements and Author's Selected Reading

Picture researcher's acknowledgement:
My personal thanks are extended to Roland Huntford, Jan Piggott and Kelly Tyler for their generous and unstinting support in helping my understanding of Sir Ernest Shackleton and the era in which he lived. I greatly appreciated it.

I should like to thank the following people for their help in locating pictures for this book and assisting with information for the captions: Thomas Binnie, Clive Coward, Jan Chojecki, Edward Elphick, Lucy Marston, Rhod McEwan, Terence Pepper, Richard Pitkin, Margot Riley, John Shackleton, Emma Strouts and Johnny Van Haeften.

For additional assistance I thank Robert Headland, Christina Leung, David McLean, Anna Shorrock, Stella Smith, Simon Steele and Joanna Wright.

Publisher's acknowledgement:
Weidenfeld & Nicolson would like to thank the many people who helped prepare this book and in particular Jan Piggott and Charles Swithinbank.

Author's selected reading:
AMUNDSEN, ROALD E.G., *The South Pole*, translated from Norwegian by A.G. Chater, John Murray, London, 1912; new edition: Cooper Square Press, New York, 2001

HUNTFORD, ROLAND, *Scott and Amundsen*, Weidenfeld & Nicolson, London, 1993; new edition: Abacus, London, 2002
Shackleton, Hodder and Stoughton, London, 1985; new edition: Abacus, London, 1996

HURLEY, FRANK, Argonauts of the South, G.P. Putnam's Sons, London, New York, 1925

HUSSEY, LEONARD, *South with Shackleton*, Sampson Low, London, 1949

LANSING, ALFRED, *Endurance* (illustrated edition), Weidenfeld & Nicolson, London, 2000

PIGGOTT, JAN (editor), *Shackleton: the Antarctic and Endurance*, Dulwich College, London, 2000

SCOTT, ROBERT F., *The Voyage of the Discovery*, Smith, Elder & Co, London, 1905; new edition: Cooper Square Press, New York, 2001

SHACKLETON, SIR ERNEST, *South*, William Heinemann, London, 1919; new edition: Penguin Books, London, 2000
The Heart of Antarctica, London, William Heinemann, 1909; new edition: London, Penguin Books, 1999

WILD, COMMANDER FRANK, *Shackleton's Last Voyage*, London, Cassell, 1923

WILSON, EDWARD A., *Diary of the Discovery Expedition to the Antarctic Regions 1901–1904*, Blandford Press, London, 1966

WORSLEY, FRANK A., *Endurance*, Philip Allan, London, 1931; new edition: W.W. Norton & Company, New York, 1999
Shackleton's Boat Journey, Philip Allan, 1933; new edition: Pimlico, London, 1999

Shackleton in London just before setting off on his final expedition, *Quest*. Leonard Hussey, who accompanied Shackleton on both *Endurance* and *Quest*, wrote to a correspondent after *Endurance*, 'Shackleton is one of the finest men I have ever met and I would follow him anywhere . . . he has always been the same – always cheerful, confident and resourceful, and at his best when things look blackest . . . what makes us admire him all the more is that he is so very human. He is a real man . . .'

First published in the United Kingdom in 2002
by Weidenfeld & Nicolson
The Orion Publishing Group
Wellington House
125 Strand
London WC2R 0BB

Text copyright © Roland Huntford 2002
Caption text copyright © Julie Summers 2002
Design and layout copyright © Weidenfeld & Nicolson 2002
Pictures copyright © *see* page 286

A CIP catalogue record for this book is available from the British Library

ISBN 0 297 84316 8

Design and art direction by David Rowley
Editorial director: Susan Haynes
Design assistance: Austin Taylor and Justin Hunt
Project manager: Caroline Brooke
Edited by Caroline Brooke and Claire Marsden
Maps by Line + Line
Picture research and captions by Julie Summers
Index by Derek Copson

Printed and bound in Italy by Printer Trento S.r.l.